Business in Mexico
Managerial Behavior, Protocol, and Etiquette

HAWORTH Marketing Resources
Innovations in Practice & Professional Services
William J. Winston, Senior Editor

New, Recent, and Forthcoming Titles:

Long Term Care Administration: The Management of Institutional and Non-Institutional Components of the Continuum of Care by Ben Abramovice

Cases and Select Readings in Health Care Marketing edited by Robert E. Sweeney, Robert L. Berl, and William J. Winston

Marketing Planning Guide by Robert E. Stevens, David L. Loudon, and William E. Warren

Marketing for Churches and Ministries by Robert E. Stevens and David L. Loudon

The Clinician's Guide to Managed Mental Health Care by Norman Winegar

Framework for Market-Based Hospital Pricing Decisions by Shahram Heshmat

Professional Services Marketing: Strategy and Tactics by F. G. Crane

A Guide to Preparing Cost-Effective Press Releases by Robert H. Loeffler

How to Create Interest-Evoking, Sales-Inducing, Non-Irritating Advertising by Walter Weir

Market Analysis: Assessing Your Business Opportunities by Robert E. Stevens, Philip K. Sherwood, and J. Paul Dunn

Marketing for Attorneys and Law Firms edited by William J. Winston

Selling Without Confrontation by Jack Greening

Persuasive Advertising for Entrepreneurs and Small Business Owners: How to Create More Effective Sales Messages by Jay P. Granat

Marketing Mental Health Services to Managed Care by Norman Winegar and John L. Bistline

Business in Mexico: Managerial Behavior, Protocol, and Etiquette by Candace Bancroft McKinniss and Arthur Natella, Jr.

Business in Mexico
Managerial Behavior, Protocol, and Etiquette

Candace Bancroft McKinniss, EdD
Arthur Natella, Jr., PhD

WARNER MEMORIAL LIBRARY
EASTERN COLLEGE
ST. DAVIDS, PA. 19087

The Haworth Press
New York • London • Norwood (Australia)

2-20-01

HF 5389 .M38 1994
McKinniss, Candace Bancroft.
Business in Mexico

© 1994 by Candace Bancroft McKinniss and Arthur Natella, Jr. All rights reserved. No part of this work may be reproduced or utilized in any form or by any means, electronic or mechanical, including photocopying, microfilm and recording, or by any information storage and retrieval system, without permission in writing from the publisher. Printed in the United States of America.

The Haworth Press, Inc., 10 Alice Street, Binghamton, NY 13904-1580

Library of Congress Cataloging-in-Publication Data

McKinniss, Candace Bancroft.
    Business in Mexico : managerial behavior, protocol, and etiquette / Candace Bancroft McKinniss, Arthur Natella, Jr.
        p.   cm.
    Includes bibliographical references and index.
    ISBN 1-56024-406-2.
    1. Business etiquette–Mexico. 2. Corporate culture–Mexico. 3. Business communication–Mexico. 4. Mexico–Foreign economic relations. I. Natella, Arthur, Jr., 1941-   . II. Title.
HF5389.M38   1994
395′.52′0972–dc20   93-23222
                                                                                             CIP

CONTENTS

ABOUT THE AUTHORS

Candace Bancroft McKinniss, EdD, is Associate Professor of Marketing (Business Administration) at Franklin Pierce College in New Hampshire. Her research and writing has focused on consumer behavior. She has had three books accepted for publication and has lectured in the areas of consumer behavior and American business at York College in England and Lincoln University in New Zealand. Dr. McKinniss has spent a number of years in business, principally in the areas of marketing research and training, working with both large companies and smaller service and not-for-profit institutions.

Arthur Natella, Jr., PhD, is head of the Spanish Department at Franklin Pierce College and Director of Intercultural/Interlanguage Consultants, a consulting agency in Keene, NH, that gives lectures and workshops on doing business in Latin America. He has published three books and given presentations on Latin American literature and culture at numerous conferences, including international symposia in Madrid, Paris, and Mexico City. Dr. Natella has been a consultant to the government of Venezuela and Co-Director of Mena International Corporation, an international marketing company specializing in US-Mexican trade.

Preface

It may not be too bold to state that the cultural contacts between Mexico and the English-speaking world have prepared both countries poorly for the important relations which will be expanding and developing as a result of the North American Free Trade Agreement. Historically, both countries have too often looked at each other with mutual distrust while their social patterns have done more to separate them than to unite them. Specifically, there is a great deal of ignorance of Mexico and of the rest of Latin America in the English-speaking world and this ignorance tends to feed on itself in the development of unfortunate cultural stereotypes that have grown up around the Mexican culture, which I am afraid are already deeply rooted in the minds of citizens of some other countries.

We are living in an age of transition, however, and such ignorance and such stereotypes can no longer stand the test of the real intercultural contact which already exists and which will accelerate greatly in the years to come. In short, we live in a globalized world in which cultures and economies are interdependent. We can no longer live in nationalistic isolation, rather we must increase and redouble our efforts to break down the walls of ignorance and cultural blindness which have separated nations since the beginning of recorded history.

The task, then, for business leaders, academics, and government officials of all countries will be to instruct their fellow countrymen on the subtleties of this increasingly interdependent international society. A new global awareness and sensitivity will have to be created based on a real appreciation of history and tradition as well as psychology and the heritage of art and literature which exists in every developed country.

It is my belief that Professors McKinniss and Natella have taken the lead in such an endeavor, attempting to delineate the Mexican psychology as well as the complexity of its culture in both an academic and eminently practical guidebook that will be of immense help both to students of international business as well as practicing businessmen and women. They have taken on a formidable task and they have carried it to conclusion with admirable skill which shows their deep knowledge of their subject.

Certainly all who are engaged in international business in Mexico can only benefit from this unique and indispensable volume, and it is to be hoped that this work will find its way into the hands of many who would wish to enter into commercial relations with Mexico on the basis of an open mind bolstered by sensitivity and true cultural awareness of the country they will be visiting.

Claudio Trulin
President, Mexican National College of Business Administration
and
Professor Emeritus of Business Administration
National University of Mexico

Chapter 1

Introduction: The Human Side

United States business is entering into a new global era in which a knowledge of foreign languages and foreign cultures is becoming increasingly important. Traditionally, U.S. citizens believe their language and culture set the world standard–to conduct business and professional matters in a responsible way is to conduct them the "American way." Now, however, with the increased competition of other countries and the economic ascendancy of other parts of the world, U.S. citizens must realize that this shrinking world brings about greater contact among people and widely divergent cultures.

CULTURAL VALUES

The result, most recently, is a United States obsession with Japan and the Japanese way of doing business. U.S. citizens often focus on the superficial aspects of Japanese techniques without a full realization that these techniques are the result of a radically different Japanese culture. Likewise, the cultural differences between the U.S. and Latin America are profound and significant. They have arisen as a result of centuries of divergent cultural patterns. In the case of Mexico, it is tempting for U.S. citizens to dismiss such differences as "underdevelopment." After all, some think, Mexico cannot be as different as other more distant parts of the world since it is a neighbor readily influenced by the cultural and business modalities of its northern business partner. Then, as Mexico does become more industrial, such differences will disappear as a more pragmatic business ethic takes place south of the border.

While it is true that there is a direct influence of business philosophy running from north to south, it is also true that profound cultural differences exist between all of Latin America, including Mexico, and the rest of North America. At the same time, these differences can present even more of an obstacle to U.S. citizens precisely because they are often not as visibly different or exotic as cultural differences between the U.S. and other countries (for example, the Middle and Far East). Yet, in their totality, these cultural differences between the United States and Latin America are vast, and it is important for businesspeople to realize that such differences are not simply arbitrary custom or habit, rather they are rooted in centuries of profound social and historical realities.

If U.S. citizens are to ever understand the nature of business in Mexico, they will not learn it from a travel book or a list of gestures and expressions that can be manipulated or changed at will. On the contrary, people from the United States will have to take the time to study and appreciate the complexity and profundity of Mexican culture as it has developed over centuries.

THE FAMILY

The family is the basis of society and U.S. citizens trying to begin to understand Mexican culture may have difficulty identifying with and understanding the depth and complexity of Mexican family values. Unlike the United States, which has a longstanding tradition of centering social roles on the individual, Mexican family values are paramount. Mexicans say that one's family is, simply, the most important thing in the world.

Mexicans usually grow up in a strong, closely-knit family unit and the family is the basic unit of Mexican society. Here the concept of family must be interpreted in the broadest sense, including not only parents and children, but also grandparents, aunts, uncles, and cousins. Likewise, other relatives may be included in the residential family: a widowed parent, a married son or daughter and his/her spouse, etc.

Whether ethnically Indian, Mestizo, or Spanish, the father is the head of the family. *Machismo*, or the cult of the power of the male, is basic to Hispanic society, and because of this the Latin family usually includes a strong father figure who dominates the family unit. The authority of the mother is also very important.

In Indian cultures, there is no leisure class and adults and children of both sexes work. By the age of six or seven most children have some work responsibilities in their home or in home industry. They accompany their family to market and fiestas and the whole family is united in work and play.

Children respect and obey their parents and, likewise, godparents are very important in the Mexican family structure. The relationship between the parents and godparents is very strong. While godparents play a direct role during baptism, confirmation, weddings, new house ceremonies, and so forth, their indirect role may be of even more importance.

In Mayan culture, for example, the godparents for the first/eldest child will generally remain godparents for all the rest of the children. To change godparents is considered a social sin. Specifically, the first choice of Mayan parents is the father and mother of the husband. If neither is alive, the wife's parents are selected. If there are no grandparents, a respected couple in the community is asked to take on the role. As a result, Mexicans care deeply about their family and about the ramifications that their individual actions will have on the whole family.

Although the family is very important in the United States, as well, many social commentators have noted that individualism seems to be a more dominant characteristic. Indeed it is very possible that this traditional emphasis given to individual needs and desires has become more pronounced in recent years with the increased importance on the so-called "me culture" in the United States. This has been exemplified by expressions such as "Do your own thing" and popular books preaching about the importance of individual desires and needs over family and the rest of society.

Many social critics have said that the United States has been developing into an increasingly personalistic and individualistic culture as traditional social and community values seem to be fading away. The result has been the increasing attention given to immediate self-gratification, often at the expense of larger social groups that surround the individual.

In contrast with this drive toward immediate self-gratification and the need for ever more consumer goods, commentators on cultural perspectives have noted the contrast between this culture of "becoming" with other cultures that tend to emphasize the culture of "being." This is to say that a country such as the United States puts a high value on personal as well as national transition–it is always in the state of becoming something else, supposedly something better, while Mexican culture pays more attention to the moment and the human interactions that are at hand.

While such generalizations must be handled with great care, lest they lend themselves to unfortunate and inaccurate stereotypes, the implications for such a cultural difference are immense, both on the personal and national level. In business, for example, cultural differences may easily translate into a less generalized materialism and a less rigid work ethic with the corresponding change in personal motivation.

Though it would be a mistake not to mention that consumerism and the materialistic society that creates such attitudes has had a profound influence in many parts of the world, it would also be a mistake to believe that all cultures have changed to adopt such values wholeheartedly or are in the process of being completely Americanized. Nevertheless there have been social changes in recent years, particularly among Mexican middle-class families. Women work and, with a rise in the education level of women in urban areas, women attend universities and many now hold responsible jobs in government and private sectors.

It is not unusual for a Mexican middle-class child to have attended summer camp, high school, and college in the U.S. Most families report having vacationed north of the border on at least two different occasions. From tourist resorts in Mexico, many have been exposed and are accustomed to U.S. styles and taste and so Halloween and Santa Claus are practiced along with the Day of the Dead and gifts from the Baby Jesus on Christmas Eve.

In Mexico, the strength and profundity of family traditions and social connections has real importance in business and professional life. While businesspeople from the U.S. are products of a technocracy in which more importance can be given to the professional qualifications than to family background, Mexicans tend to give greater importance to family associations and connections. As a result Mexicans give more importance to judging a person they meet on the basis of his or her *cultura*, referring to outward signs of breeding and good manners as well as general knowledge of culture. U.S. citizens, on the other hand, with their extremely pragmatic and individualistic bent, tend to judge people on the basis of their education or professional position alone. Likewise, by not valuing personal relationships and connections as much as Mexicans, U.S. citizens often assume that they will get an interview with a Mexican business or professional counterpart simply on the strength of a company name.

With experience in Mexican society, however, U.S. businesspeople have found that Mexicans may be less likely to speak to strangers on an impromptu basis without knowing who recommended them and who they know in their office or field. While personal connections are, of course, important anywhere in the world, networks of associations and recommendations are especially important in Mexican business and professional life.

MALE-FEMALE RELATIONS

A discussion of male-female relations in Mexico should probably begin with a discussion of marriage. Marriage, according to Catholic morality, is a lifetime arrangement. However, a double moral standard exists between the fidelity expectations placed upon males and females. Because a woman's principal obligation is to make a home and procreate, she is dedicated to a life of service and no infidelity on her part is tolerated. Even though Mexican women joined their husbands in battle during the Revolution (cooking, caring for wounds, and conducting burials), they were not granted suffrage until 1953 and were regularly instructed as to how to vote by their husbands.

Even with all the changes brought about in Mexico by its women's movement, men tend to be very jealous of their working wives and fear humiliation. They also fear that their wives may become attracted to others and become less dependent on them economically and intellectually. Most marital problems reported for middle-class families stem from the professional interests of the wives more than philandering.

As a result, Mexico is a country with different standards for different family roles. Women are expected to remain pure and pass culture on to the next generation, however, in cities and in the north, women are increasingly expected to work in home industry or outside the home in order to bring in a second income. Men are the providers: they put up with the hazards and treachery of the outside world in order to provide for their families, and expect that they will be rewarded at home for their efforts.

Because of the culture of *machismo*, businesswomen, when traveling alone, can expect the likelihood of unwelcome sexual advances: overly long eye contact, the pressing of legs under a table, and overemphasis on how appealing one looks. Like men from the U.S., Mexican men often expect to be turned down and the assumption that it was no more than a flirtation and not "truly" intended is the easiest refusal. Women should also note that Mexican men, with their deep tans and handsome European fashions, may be very attractive, but just as in the U.S., one cannot expect to entertain a sexual relationship and be taken seriously in the boardroom.

Women should take care not to entertain a man alone, as on a date, but should do so in a group. One woman explained that, upon arriving at her hotel, she introduced herself to and tipped the concierge, manager, and bell captain, explained who she was, where she was from, the length of her stay, and her business plans. As a result, she got tremendous service and a lot of helpful attention.

THE STRUCTURE OF SOCIETY

Anyone who spends a good deal of time in Mexico arrives at the conclusion that there is not one Mexico, but many. The country was first organized as a result of a series of markets. These markets were the only places in which trade was conducted. Everything was sold there, from foodstuffs to the finest cloths and from jewels to slaves. Different goods were kept in separate sections, as is the case in department stores today. The Aztecs had fixed days for the market and laws forced people to attend these market days with their wares, actually fining them for selling their goods along the way.

These markets became both commercial and social entities. One met, made friends, and socialized there. In time, these commercial centers grew into what we now see as regions, with distinct geographies, economic bases, social attitudes, and popular attributes.

The Central Highlands

The central highlands supply Mexico City with food, cheap labor, and industrial products. Indian languages include Nahuatl, Otomí and Mazahua. Cities beside Mexico City include the resort city of Cuernavaca; Puebla, a beautiful colonial city known especially for its tiles; and Toluca, a new business and industrial center.

Indian tribes in the highlands include the Otomi, the Totonac, and the Nahua, who are the largest Indian group in Mexico today. All three tribes are well known for their weaving which is sometimes in evidence in ceremonial clothing, especially sarapes. It is also not unusual to see women, particularly older ones, in colorful, handwoven woolen skirts, tied with bright sashes.

Mexico City is the world's largest urban center. It is a modern, sophisticated city 7,400 feet above sea level and ringed by mountains and volcanos. Mexico City is estimated to have a population of 20 million people and it is thought that its population will increase to 30 million by the end of the century.

Mexico City reflects the past with its numerous, colorful traditional neigborhoods which still retain their colonial character. It also looks to the future with its modern high-rise office buildings and elegant apartments.

Above all, the city is a center for an ever-increasing tempo of international business as Mexico continues to open itself up to international trade. It has become an important center for fine restaurants and upscale shops that cater to an international clientele. The city houses great archaeological treasures found in its many museums.

In recent years Mexico City has struggled with the problems of increasing competition for human space, particularly on its crowded highways, and with pollution. The current, farsighted administration of President Salinas de Gortari, has made great strides in solving problems in both areas however. All in all, Mexico City is a fascinating city that presents ever-increasing opportunities for the development of international business.

Guadalajara

Guadalajara is the second largest city in the country and it is the capital of the state of Jalisco. Other important cities include Colima, Nayarit, and Michoacán. The natives, called *Tapatíos*, are well known for their hospitality and easy-going approach to life as much as for their great pride in their local culture. Painter José Clemente Orozco and writers Juan Rulfo and Augustín Yañez all hail from Guadalajara.

This city and its surrounding areas are especially popular with American tourists and retirees who often settle at Lake Chapala and tend to stay isolated from the locals.

Veracruz

Veracruz is located on the Gulf Coast. Its most important industry is steel. Veracruz is more influenced by Cuba than the rest of Latin America, and the region produces dark coffee and strong cigars. The music and food, as well as a pre-Lenten carnival, is also very Cuban.

The oil workers' union is located in Ciudad Madero, near Tampico, and oil, energy, water, land, and agricultural resources for overcrowded conditions in the central highlands are all extremely important to the country.

The North

Like U.S. pioneers of a century ago, inhabitants of the north view their region as the "new Mexico," and feel separate, almost alienated, from the central part of the country. They perceive a real difference between themselves and the *"Chilangos"* of Mexico City.

In recent years the border areas have attracted investment capital from all parts of the world, especially in the expansion of twin (U.S. and Mexican) plants, or Maquiladoras that manufacture part of their products in the U.S. and part in Mexico. As a result the border region offers some of the most important industrial growth opportunities in the Western Hemisphere, if not in the world as a whole.

The population of cities such as Ciudad Juarez has boomed as has the economy of the north in general. Mexicans in this part of the country are proud of their economic success.

While Mexico is sometimes accused of wanting to become the fifty-first state, the *Norteños*, like U.S. Southwesterners, often feel that the central government is out of touch with its needs and is more apt to instruct than accept instructions. As a result, perhaps, the ruling PRI's (Independent Revolutionary Party) opposition, the National Action Party (PAN) has been especially strong in this part of the country in recent years.

The states of this region, Sonora, Chihuahua, Coahuila, and Durango include some of the country's best agricultural areas that provide winter fruit and vegetables, rice, wheat, and sorghum.

Monterrey

Monterrey is the second largest industrial center and the third largest city. This bustling, dynamic city comprises the industrial heart of Mexico, controlled by the Garza and Sada families, known as the Monterrey Group. Beginning with a family brewery, the Group expanded into steel, glass, chemicals, and finance.

The *Regiomontanos*, or residents of this region, see themselves as no-nonsense industrialists, although inside Mexico their reputation for thriftiness is not unlike the British stereotype of the Scots.

The South: Yucatán

The rebellious Mayans dominate Yucatán, the *Mestizos* are of mixed Spanish and Indian ancestry. The residents of the Yucatán, who call themselves *Yucatecos*, sometimes refer to the state as The Republic of Yucatán, with tongue in cheek, but the area is isolated and Merida, the capital was not connected to the national railroad system until 1950. The people tend to be stocky, with large heads and receding foreheads, having distinctively Mayan aquiline noses. As a result, they appear to be dignified, if not stubborn, and are sometimes characterized as being distrustful of outsiders (as the central government is distrustful of them).

The South: Oaxaca

Oaxaca, also in the south, has a large and highly fragmented Indian population comprised of the Mixtec, known for trade in jade and gold, and the Zapotec, including the Chatino, which is the largest Indian group in Oaxaca. The Zapotecs speak a number of different languages and/or dialects and do not generally consider themselves of one tribe, but identify more closely with their particular town or zone.

These larger groups are joined by the Mazatec, the Amuzgo, and the Tequistlatec, each of whom have their own language. The Mazatec are known for using hallucinogenic mushrooms for healing, have elaborate stories of creation, and are acknowledged for their extreme wit and insightfulness.

The indigenous population is principally employed in agriculture and tends to seem more exotic, in dress and custom, than do many other groups. Native/customary dress is seen more frequently in these parts.

Oaxaca is made up of 570 municipalities, many of which are very old, pre-Conquest cities. The state has seen a good deal of violence over communal land rights and the eroded hills are not able to sustain the corn crop needed. Migration to Puebla and Mexico City is not uncommon.

A good deal of anthropological research has been done on the native population in this region. This region is considered a rebellious one, angry and competitive. It is also one in which a good deal of stereotypical *machismo* exists.

The South: Chiapas

Chiapas, with its overflow of immigrant Guatemalan Indians, provides a buffer between Mexico and Central America. Until 1830, Chiapas was part of Guatemala and, with its mountains and lakes, it looks more like Guatemala than Oaxaca. Principal crops include coffee and cotton, grown on plantations. A strategic highway developed through the Lacandon jungle along the Mexican/Guatemalan border–a result of the 1984 Guatemalan intrusion to capture Guatemalan refugees–will open the area for oil exploration and the construction of hydroelectric dams, leading to development.

The Mayan Lancandons are stereotyped as having long, flowing hair and ankle-length tunics, and using bark cloth and hand looms. While feared by their distant Mayan relatives in the south, they tend to be gentle people with solid religious and intellectual traditions. The Tzeltaltan Mayans are from the central highlands of Chiapas and are traditionally farmers. Many have become truck farmers and migrant workers and are divided into two geographic and linguistic groups, the Tzotzil and the Tzeltal.

The central government has recently issued $900 million for new schools, health clinics, nutrition, and road construction programs throughout the southeast: Chiapas, Oaxaca, Veracruz, Tabasco, Campeche, Yucatán, and Quintana Roo. This should result in some dramatic changes in both the acculturation and deculturation of this region.

POPULAR CULTURE

While a good deal of Mexican society has become deculturated, many of Mexico's cultural roots have remained deeply embedded in day-to-day existence. Music, dance, art, architecture, and literature have maintained strong ties to classic Mexico, although some of the more common forms of mass entertainment, television, movies, and radio, have not.

A number of national composers have made global contributions, including Silvestre Revueltas, Carlos Chavez, Manuel Ponce, and José Pablo Moncayo. The Mexico City Orchestra is a world-class symphony orchestra.

Dance is very important in Mexico. It is important to note the work of Amalia Hernández and the Folkloric Ballet Company.

Painting has emphasized colorful, day-to-day themes (realism) and, of the 15,000 painters, engravers, and sculptors, a few major contributors come to mind. Their contributions can be found in Mexico's many museums and galleries: Rivera, Siqueiros and Orozco; Juan O'Gorman, Frida Kahlo, Pablo O'Higgins, and Dr. Atl (Gerardo Murillo); the satirical engraver, José Guadalupe Posada; and Oaxacan surrealists Tamayo and Francisco Toledo. Merida's abstract art is not unlike pre-Columbian archaeological findings. Colorful works like those from Pedro Coronel, Ricardo Martínez and Luiz López Loza are considered distinctly Mexican.

Until the end of the Mexican Revolution of 1910, architecture followed a traditional style of churrigueresque facades, thick adobe walls, archways and staircases, elegant balconies looking to inner patios and hidden gardens, and so forth. Díaz encouraged a more neo-baroque style exemplified in the Palace of Fine Arts, the new Congress building, and the Monument to the Revolution. Pedro Ramírez Vázquez's reinforced concrete design can be seen at the National University, the National Museum of Anthropology and Aztec Stadium. Ruiz Barragán influenced the design of private residences with reflecting pools, hidden gardens, freestanding walls, and vivid colors.

Mexico may have made some of its greatest contributions to world culture through its literature. Early literary contributors include playwright Juan Ruiz de Alarcón; the seventeenth-century nun, Sister Juana Inés de la Cruz, who wrote poetry and drama; and more recent poets, Ramón López Velarde and José Juan Tablada. Postrevolutionary novelists include Mariano Azuela, whose classic of the Mexican revolution, *Los de abajo* (*The Underdogs*), has been widely translated and made into a film. Other important twentieth-century authors include Xavier Villaurrutia, José Gorostiza, and Salvador Novo. Mexico's well-known international novelists include Juan Rulfo and Carlos Fuentes, as well as José Revueltas, Vincente Leñero, Jorge Ibarguengöitia, Gustavo Sainz, and Carlos Monsivais, to mention only a few. Carlos Pellicer should join Nobel Prize-winning Octavio Paz, Alí Chumacero, José Emilio Pacheco, and Homero Arvidjis in a list of important modern poets. Political cartoonist Eduardo del Río is penned Rius, and is read almost as widely as the popular Luis Spota. Not well known outside of Mexico, Spota's novels sell 50,000 or more copies routinely.

The movie industry is controlled by the government. Traditional movies were didactic in nature and offered stories of the Virgin of Guadalupe, Emiliano Zapata, Pancho Villa, and other revolutionary heroes. Musical melodramas were popular during the industry's Golden Era in the 1930s and 1940s and they generally focused on the Mexican *charro* (cowboy). World-renowned figures were involved in making these films, including cameraman Gabriel Figueroa (who shot for Luis Brunel); directors Emilio Fernández, Julio Bracho, and Fernando de Fuente; actresses Dolores del Río and María Félix; actors Pedro Armendariz and Mario Moreno; and singers Jorge Negrete, Pedro Infante, and Javier Solís. During the Echeverría period, 1970-76, the government took a greater interest in filmmaking and Mexico produced directors Felipe Cazals, Gustavo Alatrist, Paul Leduc, Alberto Isaac, Arturo Ripstein, and Alfonso Arau.

Mexican music was extremely popular in the 1930s and 1940s and the country used its movies as a vehicle for its music (Jorge Negrete, Pedro Infante, Javier Solís). Mariachi music is always popular, while "New" music tends to imitate Caribbean salsa, U.S. rock, and Argentinean/Chilean protest music.

THE MEXICAN HERITAGE

Indeed it may be extremely difficult for U.S. citizens, without prior knowledge of Latin American or Hispanic culture, to appreciate the depth of pride that Mexicans have in their country, traditions, and families. Mexico is proud of both its Hispanic and Indian heritage. This Hispanic tradition goes back to Spain, a country whose principal language sprang from the Latin language while the Arab culture coexisted in Spain for some 700 years. As a result, 6,000 words in the Spanish language originated in Arabic. At the same time, Arab culture made profound contributions to Spanish culture in the areas of literature, science, architecture, mathematics, and philosophy. Although there are certainly many other reasons why family values have been important in the Hispanic world, the deep bonds of Arab familial life certainly have to rank high on the list.

Indian heritage is also basic to an understanding of all of Latin America. It is important to realize that just about all traditional societies, including Mexican Indian societies, were based on the family, tribe, or clan as the basic societal unit. Individual rights were generally secondary to the rights and interests of the larger tribal group itself. Although tribes such as the Aztecs and Mayans are well-known parts of Mexico's illustrious past, it is not generally known that hundreds of different tribes with their unique languages and cultures were and still are an important part of Mexican culture.

The history of the indigenous people is a long and elaborate one. By 3500 B.C., 40,000 years after crossing the Bering Strait, the people stopped being nomadic and started to cultivate the land. Corn, which is still vitally important in the Mexican diet, replaced wild fruit and hunted animals, and assumed a religious significance as the source of life.

The Olmecs (1200 B.C.) were the first important civilization in Mexico. They settled in the coastal areas of the Gulf of Mexico, southern Veracruz, and Tabasco. There are three important Olmec cities: La Venta, San Lorenzo, and Tres Zapotes. The Olmecs are known for their great artistic achievements and religious sensitivity. They also developed the concept of zero, unknown to their Roman contemporaries, and a sophisticated dating system. In short, their influence was not through war, but through trade and religion. No tribe existing today can be traced to the Olmecs.

The Mayans (1500 B.C.), settled in the Yucatán, Guatemala, Belize, and to some degree, the Honduras, and El Salvador. By 150 B.C. their first city states emerged in the central lowland, El Pelen, and Guatemala. Tikal was the architectural, jewelry, and religious center, but by 900 A.D. this area was abandoned and the center was moved to Yucatán (Palenque, Uxmal, Chictien Itza, Tulum). By 1200 A.D. the Mayan Empire consisted of dozens of different tribes, city-states, dialects, costumes, religious rituals, and gods, and was held together by politics, language, trade, and religion.

The Zapotecs are the first tribe recorded in Oaxaca in 300 B.C., in the city of Monte Albán. They dominated Mexico for 900 years. Monte Alban was abandoned for Zaachila, but the Mixtecs used Monte Albán as their ceremonial cemetery.

The Aztec culture dominated the center of Mexico and its capital, Teotihuacán, was estimated to be the most populous city of the world at the height of the Aztec culture. Huge pyramids dedicated to the Sun and Moon deities and a two-mile long Avenue of the Dead were centers of the city. This city was something of a melting pot and this is where the famous Quetzalcoatl, the Plumed Serpent, invented medicine, agriculture, astronomy, and royalty.

According to legend the Aztecs were originally a nomadic

people. However, they were told by their gods that they were to settle in an area where they would see an eagle with a writhing serpent in its beak. The Aztecs did settle in this area with modern-day Mexico City being the site of their major city. This symbol is seen today in coins and in the flag of Mexico.

This Aztec city was composed of islands of *chinampas* (floating gardens), linked to each other and the mainland by broad causeways and two aqueducts. Farmers and traders walked or canoed daily to Tenochtitlán to spread their wares in front of the huge palace of the Emperor and the Great Temple (Templo Mayor). In 1502 Montezuma II, Emperor and High Priest of Huitziloposhtli, ruled, feasting daily on fish and wearing richly woven robes, fine jewelry, and a feathered headdress.

Indian culture still has a great influence on the main hallmarks of Mexican society. Most of Mexico's population has some Indian blood, and Indian influence can still be seen almost everywhere in Mexico from architecture, art, literature, handicrafts, and language to the basic view of the world. The Indian culture, although vastly different from one society to another, often tends to believe that destiny is predetermined by the gods, customs are established by ancestors and monitored by their spirits. Problems are solved by shamans and discipline is maintained by elders.

To what extent Mexican culture is still defined by its indigenous past has been a basic controversy among Mexican intellectuals such as Samuel Ramos, Carlos Fuentes, Octavio Paz and others. One of the most provocative theories relating to Mexican psychology is that of Octavio Paz, who states in his famous book, *The Labyrinth of Solitude*, that the Mexican has a deep-seated inferiority complex based on the conquest of native Indian culture, particularly the Aztec culture, by the Spaniards. Paz theorizes that the Mexican attempts to make up for a sense of inferiority by outwardly displaying strength and forcefulness or *machismo*. As a consequence of this Mexicans often hide their true feelings behind a mask, seen by Paz as being exemplified in the classic of the Mexican theater, *El gesticulador*–a drama written by the twentieth-century dramatist Rodolfo Usigli, in which a historian becomes a national hero of Mexico as he takes on the identity of a dead hero from the Mexican revolution.

Paz's theories are highly controversial and are seen by many Mexicans as applying mainly to the inhabitants of Mexico City, the place where Hernán Cortez conquered the Aztec civilization. What is generally agreed on, however is that Mexico's indigenous past has had a determining influence on its modern society. Indeed, the Mexican Revolution of 1910 was not only a political revolution but a social one as well in terms of that country's ability to come to grips with its own past. As a result of this popular movement, Mexican society drew less of its cultural identity from Europe and began to dig deeper into the mysterious and profound ground of its indigenous past. After this historical event, handicrafts, literature and sculpture, among other manifestations of culture, began to show a decidedly Indian influence, whereas nineteenth century high culture of Mexico was often considered successful to the degree in which it imitated European models.

The ascendancy of the PRI or *Partido Revolucionario Independiente* (Independent Revolutionary Party) after the Mexican Revolution brought with it Mexico's famous and influential muralistic school of artists such as Diego Rivera and José Clemente Orozco. Both artists mirrored the Indian tendency to value the group over the individual in paintings and murals, often portraying large masses of humanity as the dominating focal point over traditional European works focusing on the individual.

These concepts are all the more important for our understanding of Mexican society since Mexicans themselves are keenly aware of the development of these currents in their history and culture. In contrast, it has often been said that U.S. citizens are a people without history in the sense that, compared to other countries and cultures, people in the U.S. seem to feel that historical developments have little bearing on their lives and on modern day life in general. This is, of course, a very broad generalization, yet to the extent that it may be true, it can lead U.S. businesspeople to believe that it is not important for them to understand the history of a country that they want to conduct business in. The belief that just the opposite is true cannot be emphasized too strongly since it is an important part of the basic philosophy of this book.

Though Mexicans are keenly aware of the cultural differences of inhabitants of their own country, they, like many foreigners, can be unaware of the vast cultural differences within the United States and they often believe that the U.S. citizen is just one cultural commodity. In effect, negative stereotyping is a problem for people on both sides of the border and Mexicans often consider U.S. citizens to be overly cold, insensitive, boorish, and extremely provincial in their dealings with foreigners.

It can be clearly seen that the cultural identity of Mexico is extremely diverse and an understanding of Mexican psychology is a real challenge for those in business who approach life from a radically different standpoint. Such differences have important ramifications for all areas of international business including, but not limited to marketing, management, international negotiations, arbitration, and law. In addition, interpersonal relations often involve complicated social differences in written and oral communication, different conventions relating to gifts, social invitations, and clothing, as well as a whole host of other issues.

Within the climate of today's ever-shrinking world, attention to these matters, which may have been considered by businesspeople as purely social matters, are becoming extremely important. In effect, we have come to realize, more than ever before, that business is not simply a mechanical matter. Business is conducted by people and it succeeds to the degree that people succeed in their relations and negotiations with one another. To the degree that they can come to agreement on the principles and practices that make up their individual endeavors they will be successful.

Chapter 2

A Political and Economic History of Mexico

An overview of Mexican history will lead to a deeper understanding of some of the differences between Mexicans and U.S. citizens. Additionally, it should provide an appreciation of both the rich contribution of Mexico's indigenous past and an awareness of the political and social contributions of the Spaniards. It is, perhaps, easiest to appreciate the development of Mexican business if one begins chronologically.

PRE-COLUMBIAN MEXICO

While evidence exists to suggest human life near Puebla around 30,000 to 40,000 years ago, excavators found evidence of the earliest farming cultures functioning from 7000 to 6000 B.C. As animal populations thinned, nomadic hunters became more sedentary and sought an agricultural existence. Complex civilizations grew during the Archaic Period (5000 to 1500 B.C.). Archaeologists have found baskets from this period and evidence of pottery exists as early as 2400 B.C. Additionally, they have found evidence of corn, beans, squash, tomatoes, turkeys, and dogs. The main crop, maize or corn, remains a staple of the Mexican diet.

Archaeolgical data from 2000 B.C. to 300 A.D. also suggests that a strong farming culture continued. Farming was done either by using the "slash and burn" method of cutting grass and trees and setting fire to the cleared area, or by constructing irrigation ducts and terraces. Irrigation systems were located principally in the highlands around Mexico City, where the first large towns developed.

From 300-900 A.D., life centered around cities and it appears that this is where class distinctions arose. A class of merchants and artisans grew. Farmers, previously independent, became serfs under a landlord's control. During the first part of this period Maya came to rival contemporary Europe in the areas of engineering, mathematics, astronomy, and calendrical calculations. Architecture and artwork were extremely sophisticated. The cultural centers of this period were the Yucatán and Guatemala (Mayan); the Mexican Highlands (at Teotihuacán); Monte Albán and Mitla (Zapotec cities near Oaxaca); and Tajín and Zempoala (Totonac cities on the Gulf Coast).

The following period, 900-1520, was typical of wartime, and there was a good deal of migration. In the 1300s the Aztecs settled in the Mexico Valley on Lake Texcoco (Mexico City). Their capital, the island city of Tenochtitlán, grew to become one of the world's largest cities (population 300,000). The empire developed from a loosely united group of states and territories and the high lords became fabulously rich in gold, stores of food, cotton, and perfumes. Artisans were prosperous and *chinampas*, (floating gardens), allowed the Aztecs to efficiently cultivate the swamplands.

THE COLONIAL PERIOD

Cortez landed in 1519 in the area now known as Veracruz. Montezuma, who immediately saw the Spanish as a threat to his control, bribed Cortez and his men to leave. However, the gold only served to encourage the greedy Spanish to remain.

Mexico and the rest of Latin America was part of the Spanish empire for centuries and it is notable that Latin America was first developed by large landowners who were, in effect, feudal lords. Such *señores* held vast tracts of land that employed thousands of workers or *peones*. In Mexico, the largest of these *haciendas* (estates) were larger than many present-day U.S. states. The result, of course, was that the power and influence of the owners of these estates was immense, not only in their own areas of the country, but in national politics as well.

Because the Colonial Period was one of Spanish lords and feudal estates, Spain prospered from Mexico's natural resources. Mexican land, silver, and gold made Spain the richest country in Europe and this feudal arrangement lasted well into the twentieth century.

Mexico was also a center of culture in the new world, as the Catholic Church brought formal European-style education to the new continent. The result of all this has markedly affected Mexican society, giving it a more hierarchical, less democratic view of life with authority coming from a strong central figure.

INDEPENDENCE FROM SPAIN

The Mexican independence movement began in 1810 when Father Miguel Hidalgo preached independence in Dolores, Guanajuato. Hidalgo sought help from a military officer, Ignacio de Allende, and they were joined by Father José María Morelos. While that revolt failed and Hidalgo was executed, he is honored as Mexico's foremost patriot. Morelos kept the revolt alive until his own execution in 1815.

A primitive textile industry had started during the Colonial Period and was all but lost during the independence movement. However, Lucas Alamán modernized it and, in 1830, developed the Banco de Avío, the country's first national bank offering credit to promote industrial growth and agricultural development.

From 1821 (independence) through 1860, four constitutional systems were established, two centralist and two federalist. A number of elected officials ran the government, most of whom were assassinated, including Augustín de Iturbide and President Vicente Guerrero, who had both authored the independence. Only Guadalupe Victoria (1825-1829), the head of the first federalist republic, and José Joaquín de Gerrera (1848-1851), ruler during the second federalist republic held full terms. From the Plan of Veracruz (December 6, 1822) through the Plan of Ayutla (March 1, 1854) Antonio López de Santa Anna (officially president 1853-1855) dominated the national government and Lucas Alamán, in his history of Mexico, dubbed this period, "the history of the revolutions of Santa Anna."

Even though the dictatorship of Santa Anna ran throughout the period of Mexico's independence (Iturbide's Plan of Iguala) and

Mexico's separation from Spain, formal independence did not greatly alter the political status quo.

Santa Anna's reign could best be described as a period of continuous civil war. The country had to be saved from a reconquest by Spain that was supported by the Holy Alliance. Britain allied itself with Spain, while the U.S., through the Monroe Doctrine, aided Mexico. However, the U.S. took advantage of Santa Anna's defeat at San Jacinto in 1836 to annex Texas in 1845. The Mexican War (U.S.-Mexican) in 1847 left some international doubts about Mexico's ability to defend itself.

Following a 33-year period of anarchy, Mexico arrived at the Constitution of 1857, strengthened by the reform laws of 1859, and secular civil power, greater than that of the Church, was established. A number of minor dictators continued to rule Mexico until the 1860s when Napoleon III of France offered the Archduke Maximilian of Habsburg the crown of Mexico as a puppet emperor. This rule lasted for three years (1864-1867) while the country was in a civil war. Napoleon III was pressured by the U.S. to withdraw his troops, and Maximilian, then abandoned by Napoleon, was captured and executed by a Mexican firing squad in Querétaro. Benito Juárez, a Zapotec Indian lawyer, the great national hero and founder of modern Mexico, succeeded Maximilian as president and did his best to unify the country until his heart attack and subsequent death in 1872.

The revolutionary liberals launched programs of reform leading to the establishment of a constitutional government, abolishing the independent powers of the clergy and military, and stimulating economic progress. As a result, Porfirio Díaz was able to offer a period in which some freedom with respect to property, labor, interest, and enterprise (e.g., modern capitalism) could become a reality.

Consumer goods production and demand grew during General Porfirio Díaz' Presidential period (1877-1911). During the long *Porfiriato* Period, government stimulated the development of heavy industry which increased demands on Mexico's mines, railways, and construction industries. During this period, the upper class prospered, foreign investments grew, and the government balanced its budget.

The Porfiriato Period can be divided into three stages. (1) Pacification existed from 1876 through 1884 whereby the country's anarchy came to rest, controlled by Díaz' show of armed force. Once his enemies were at bay, he was able to expand the economy which was spurred on by foreign capital. (2) The apogee (1855-1905) was a period when foreign investment was encouraged through legislation (June 21, 1885). This legislation allowed conversion of the foreign debt. (3) A crisis period ensued from 1905 through 1911 in which new loans (31 million pounds through mid-1911) from abroad were obtained and a climate of confidence for foreign investors occurred. Foreigners began to buy up Mexico. However, the apparent financial well-being was, for Mexico, a facade.

While self-congratulation characterized the Díaz administration, social problems were rampant. The Indians and the growing working class were neglected during the Porfiriato. Indian and Mestizo lands were confiscated and concessions to foreigners (particularly U.S. citizens) damaged the economic position of the middle class. In order to accelerate industrial growth, the government set up high tariff barriers against competing products and on June 3, 1893 it granted tax exemptions to those launching new industries.

Additionally, foreigners dominated the most important activities of the Porfirian economy. In 1911 they controlled 98 percent of the railroad shares, 97.5 percent of the petroleum shares, and 97.4 percent of the mining shares. A good deal of hostility existed against the Chinese in the north, on the part of U.S. and British economic interests.

THE MEXICAN REVOLUTION

Francisco I. Madero pulled together an alliance of peasants, workers, and the middle class before his assassination in November 1910. After the Revolution of 1910, a new constitution (1917) established the institutions that shaped the alliance, a mixed economy whereby industrialization began with the breaking up of many feudal *haciendas*. The "Constitution of 1917" guaranteed free secular education, restored land to peasants, limited property accumulation, instituted a 48-hour work week and minimum wage, and established written mandates for equal rights for women and laborers.

The Mexican Revolution also resulted in the emergence of political stability through the establishment of a single ruling party, the

Partido Revolucionario Independiente (PRI). As a result of the revolution, an industrial base, which had been predominantly agrarian, became increasingly industrial and service oriented. The gross national product multiplied five times. National production and irrigation projects allowed Mexico to feed itself and supply raw materials to industry. Mining also decreased in its importance in the economy and, with the exception of iron, mining became relatively stagnant. The railroad network increased from 431 miles in 1925 to about 30,000 miles in 1960. However, Mexico's economic development was still the result of sacrifice on the part of low-income workers.

Additionally, Mexico maintained a relatively high foreign debt, combined with domination of technology by foreign firms. Additionally, the infrastructure (petroleum, railways, electricity, etc.) was controlled by the state. A population explosion counteracted the effectiveness of policies affecting labor (e.g., minimum wage and profit sharing laws), agriculture (the *ejido*), and education (rural problems and literacy). Political stability, while a great achievement, also helped cause the country's rigidity, impeding freedom of growth and development for agriculture and labor.

Most specifically, President Plutarco Elías Calles (1928-1934) began a program of public works in the 1920s which built roads and irrigation projects. While his term was characterized by government's struggle against the Church, it was also marked by a serious conflict with the U.S. over the oil question, and the growth of power of organized labor (CROM). Calles stepped up land reform and distributed eight million hectares in 1924-1928. He built up relations with the labor confederation, invested in education, sanitation, and health.

Despite all Calles' accomplishments, land distribution slowed down during his last year in office and social programs became corrupt. Repression of the labor movement began and his popularity waned to the extent that Calles was arrested and deported in 1936 by his successor, Lázaro Cárdenas.

MEXICAN NATIONALISM

Although Mexico remained a capitalist country, President Lázaro Cárdenas (1934-1940) enacted a number of reforms. Successive governments nationalized other industries including the banks and the national telephone utility. The result has been a highly nationalistic, protectionist economy which sought to lessen international competition in favor of the support of local industries.

Cárdenas created the National Polytechnic Institute and offered a number of reforms along the lines of agrarian and labor policies. He invested heavily in education and established good relations with labor and peasant organizations. As a result, he was able to break up vast tracts of agricultural land (his government seized 49 million acres of land from private owners) and distributed parcels to small cooperative farms (*ejidos*). Since the outbreak of the revolution 26 million acres had been distributed. During Cárdenas' administration, 49 million more acres were shared out.

Cárdenas also reorganized labor unions along democratic lines and provided federal funding for village schools. His most famous action, though, was the expropriation of Mexico's oil industry from U.S. and European interests. He nationalized the 17 oil companies operating in Mexico and instituted the *Petroleros Mexicanos* (PEMEX).

Particularly concerned about social issues, Cárdenas extended the social security system but was unable to increase real wages during a period of 7.3 percent inflation. He was particularly concerned about the problems posed by rapid population growth and urbanization and in his last address to congress he recognized that economic development had taken place at the expense of social justice.

Manuel Avila Camacho, Cárdenas' successor, reorganized the *Nacional Financiera* (the International Bank of Mexico) to encourage industrialization, thus further developing the country economically and raising the standard of living. During his administration profound economic changes resulted from World War II. At that time a strong U.S. demand for Mexican minerals, metals, oil, and food developed and his administration is credited with developing transportation. After a German U-boat sunk a Mexican tanker near Florida, a number of Mexicans enlisted in the U.S. armed forces and a squadron of the Mexican air force was sent to the Pacific. In 1945 Mexico became a charter member of the United Nations.

Cárdenas had signed the Bracero Agreement in 1942, allowing

Mexican migrant workers to take jobs across the U.S. border. As a result, migration increased to the interior urban areas, as during Camacho's presidency.

Miguel Alemán Valdés (1946-1952), sometimes referred to as the "architect of modern Mexico," expanded the nation's industries and infrastructure. Alemán invested heavily in public works, principally hydroelectric power, irrigation projects, and road building. As the economy grew, so did the middle class, although there was still a concentration of wealth. Tourism also began developing at this time.

The government was conservative and kept wages behind inflation, troops were sent to break up a strike by oil workers and the administration eventually became known for large-scale corruption, especially in the area of awarding public sector contracts. In general, after the war, emphasis on reform took a back seat to industrial growth and development of the country's resources.

President Adolfo Ruiz Cortines (1952-1958), known in part for his serious effort to eliminate graft and corruption in government and his attempts to bring in economic stability, greatly extended Mexico's farmland through irrigation projects. Cortines' administration, however, was also marked by the need to devalue the peso in 1954. Foreign investment grew considerably, especially after the devaluation of the peso.

Cortines' main achievement may have been his extension of the franchise to women. The past few decades marked a period in which Mexico experienced a modern feminist movement. The United Front for Women's Rights, organized in 1935, had 50,000 members in 1940. Mexican women were awarded suffrage in 1955.

Adolfo López Mateos (1958-1964) expanded the highway system, increased hydroelectric power sources, and expanded Mexico's educational system. He accelerated the pace of land reform which had slowed significantly since the mid-1940s and during his *sexenio* (or six-year term in office), 30 million acres were distributed, second only to Cárdenas in the 1930s. The public sector expanded at this time and the state purchased majority shareholdings in a number of foreign firms, including U.S. and Canadian electric companies. He spent heavily on social welfare and made important advances in medical care, especially the control and prevention of tuberculosis, polio, and malaria. He also initiated large-scale housing programs for low-income groups and implemented clauses in the constitution calling for profit-sharing for industry workers.

Gustavo Díaz Ordaz (1964-1970) provided credit and technical help to the agricultural sector of the economy. During this time he maintained a sound rate of economic growth (average 6 percent per annum), increased spending on education and urban renewal, and was a driving force behind the signing of the Tlatelolco Treaty (the Treaty for the Prohibition of Nuclear Weapons), February 14, 1967. However, despite all of his contributions, Díaz Ordaz is remembered for the Tlatelolco massacre, the bloody repression of high school and university student protests in 1968, just before the start of the Olympic Games in Mexico City.

THE LOST YEARS

Luis Echeverría Alvarez, in 1970, followed by Jóse López Portillo in 1976 brought with them a period of widescale corruption in the upper echelons of Mexican society. Echeverría ran into widening budget deficits which encouraged inflation and capital flight. In 1976 the peso was devalued for the first time in 22 years. Just 11 days before leaving office Echeverría expropriated large tracts of private farmland in Sonora, creating speculation of a coup d'etat and one of the tensest transitions in Mexican history.

Jóse López Portillo presided over the country's oil boom and a period of rapid but unbalanced economic growth and heavy foreign borrowing that came to an abrupt end in 1982 with the foreign payment crisis. Following a drop in oil prices in mid-1981, capital flight began. In February, López Portillo was forced to devalue the peso by 40 percent and the government announced the suspension of payments on the foreign debt in August. In September he nationalized privately owned banks and imposed sweeping exchange controls. After the end of his term, the government considered prosecuting him on corruption charges. Corruption already existed, though, and may have been fostered by the fast influx of money into Mexican banks through the raising of oil prices. Oil income was one of many areas that reinforced Mexican borrowing and spending. When oil prices dropped in the 1980s, Mexico was left with an enormous debt to foreign banks and serious deficiencies in its infrastructure.

Mexicans refer to the 1970s as "the lost years." Not only was government corrupt, but large budget deficits, high unemployment, a burgeoning population, weak and lagging agricultural production, high inflation, and rapid devaluation of the peso all helped spur on tremendous economic disparity and popular dissatisfaction. As a result, Mexico found itself virtually closed to foreign investment and imports of most manufactured products. Inefficient firms were unable to supply products for export and were therefore overly reliant on the oil industry to generate foreign currency earnings to finance imports and equipment. In 1987 the inflation rate was 159 percent and the budget deficit rose to over 15 percent of the gross national product. Billions of dollars were transferred overseas by wealthy Mexicans.

Debt crisis is not a new phenomenon in Mexico. During the Baring Panic of the 1890s a number of borrowers defaulted on their bonds. However, most of the current borrowing was not from the state-owned banks–historically the source–but directly from investors. Few debtors tend to default on bonds and new borrowers are now raising equity to avoid too much debt. Also, private sector companies have begun policies of buying back debt at a discount.

While oil prices were high and the industry was growing, Mexico neglected its agricultural and industrial sectors. Now it is in the process of rebuilding theses areas, cutting government expenditures, getting control over corruption, and keeping creditors satisfied.

MEXICAN ECONOMIC REFORMS

President Miguel de la Madrid took office in 1982, only months after the country defaulted on its foreign debt payments. The economy rebounded at first as he pursued austerity policies under pressure from the International Monetary Fund. Madrid signed stand-by agreements with the IMF and rescheduled the country's commercial bank debt. Although no appreciable growth occured from January to October of 1988, the rate of inflation fell from 15 to 1 percent.

Carlos Salinas de Gortari was elected in 1988, winning under conditions of a historic low level of support for PRI against the newly formed National Democratic Front (FDN). Salinas suggested that domestic economic growth would take precedence over servicing Mexico's foreign debt. He also promised modernization of the economy, greater political pluralism, and a new emphasis on the redistribution of wealth. In short he opened Mexico to private investment and this liberalization included easing banking rules, selling state-owned businesses, and awarding construction contracts to private companies. From 1988 to 1990, the country brought in $80 billion in foreign investment.

Salinas took control of office at a time when unemployment was high, foreign debt was $105 billion (U.S.), domestic production was low, and drug transport problems left the nation and the world skeptical. His wage and price controls helped keep inflation below 20 percent and his arrests of a union boss, a fraudulent businessman, and a drug trafficker began his upsurge in national and international popularity.

President Salinas de Gortari's plan to revise the structure of the economy of Mexico includes encouraging foreign investment by revamping the core of import-export law as well as other laws. As mentioned earlier, the breakup of the vast *haciendas* and the privatization of many industries after the revolution resulted in Mexico turning inward, in a business and economic sense, and developing protectionist economic policies. This situation prevailed until recently, but foreign business is currently finding Mexico a much more favorable place to do business, as laws–such as the one limiting foreign investment in Mexico to 49 percent of ownership–have recently been struck from the books. It is expected that with the signing of the North American Free Trade Agreement (NAFTA), international investment and commerce will greatly increase in Mexico.

The economy grew by 3 percent in 1989. Inflation fell to 20 percent from 114 percent in 1988. Mexicans returned $10.7 billion to the country in 1989 and 1990, by buying internationally-traded bonds. Private sector debt fell from $23 billion in 1982 to $10 billion in 1988.

Mexico and creditor banks signed the first Brady Agreement in 1989. Banks agreed to trade in loans for secured bonds with lower face value or lower interest rates. This cut the debt burden by one-sixth and helped revive confidence in the economy. Also, two mega-bonds, called Aztec bonds, were created. They paid two times the margin over the bank's cost of funds as the old bank did. These were secured by U.S. treasury paper and were traded internationally.

While the budget deficit in 1982 was about 7 percent of Mexico's GDP, not including interest payments, a government surplus now exists. Since Salinas de Gortari took office, deep cuts in public spending have been made and state-owned companies have had to raise prices. Most subsidies have been dropped. In 1989 import quotas were eliminated and tariffs were cut to 20 percent to embrace foreign investment.

The 1992 inflation rate was 15 percent and falling and the budget was balanced. Economic growth is over 3.5 percent after inflation, indicating strong domestic investment and nonpetroleum exports. Salinas tightened monetary policy and central banking is keeping interest rates down to prevent excessive rises in the value of the Mexican peso. Government spending was cut rather than raising taxes (GNP was cut from 30 percent to under 20 percent) and subsidies were reduced to the inefficient Mexican private firms, losses in state-owned businesses were reduced, and political patronage was eliminated. The *Pacto*, an agreement between business and organized labor, limited increases in prices and wages (backed by government price controls on consumer staples) and business and labor leaders met with government officials to ensure that no political disturbances or organized resistance began. Additionally, as the inflation rate declined, most controls on prices were eliminated. Government is evolving toward the goal of letting prices and wages be determined by market conditions.

Interest rates in Mexico now are still higher than U.S. rates. The newly-signed North American Free Trade Agreement should break down many barriers to the flow of trade and capital. This, in turn, should narrow differentials in inflation and interest rates. Mexican short-term treasury bill rates, while still high, have been cut by more than half from 1991 to 1992. Additionally, the government's economic reforms are liable to hold beyond the end of Salinas' term in 1994.

Salinas' efforts to modernize the economy have made Mexico an increasingly stable, internationally competitive, market-oriented country. In fact, Mexico's economy is one of the best performing economies in the world. During the early part of Salinas' administration, Mexico paid off about one-eighth of its domestic debt. On February 4, 1990, representatives of the Mexican government and 450 foreign commercial creditors signed a debt reduction agreement designed to ease the banking crisis and decrease interest payments. The Mexican government, also, raised $7 billion through its privatization programs and the government's share of gross domestic product has been halved (from one-third to one-sixth). Interest (accounting for 50 percent of the national budget) is under 25 percent and falling. Lower interest rates cut the deficit and the private sector can enter credit markets, thereby encouraging investment.

Capital flight from Mexico had become a major problem. Since 1989, however, $9 billion in flight capital returned to Mexico and about $15 billion in foreign investment was made.

U.S. exports to Mexico from 1987 to 1990 grew from $14.6 billion to over $28.4 billion. The U.S. Commerce Department estimates that $1 billion in exports creates 22,000 jobs and so it is estimated that over 600,000 U.S. jobs are related to U.S. exports to Mexico.

A key to the success of Salinas' programs is that government is not using its proceeds for current spending but is reducing Mexico's net national debt, therefore lowering interest costs for government and eliminating subsidies previously paid to lossmaking national firms. Savings are also used to finance programs for the poor, including rural electrification and sanitation projects. Additionally, Salinas has taken steps to reduce the level of industrial air pollution.

While Salinas used privatization to make significant strides in the health of the economy, it is worthwhile to note that not everyone in Mexico supports the privatization of Mexican companies. Some still believe in a managed economy and others worry that the national *patrimonio* is being sold off. Additionally, many are also concerned about child labor. However, from 1983 to 1991 the government raised $8 billion by selling over 170 companies. Just about all of those slated for sale are now sold.

Tax reforms have also had an impact on Salinas' economy. The enforcement and jailing of cheaters has resulted in significant tax collection increases, despite a decrease in top personal income taxes from 60 to 35 percent. Corporate tax rates are down from 43 to 35 percent. A value-added tax cut was made from 15 to 10 percent.

TODAY AND TOMORROW

The economic outlook for Mexico is bright indeed. Nevertheless, Mexicans who are pleased that foreign goods are entering their country are still living with the effects of rampant inflation and constant devaluation of the peso which has led, in recent years, to inflation rates approaching 100 percent per year. For the average person this has led to price increases which make it difficult for many to afford luxury items.

Additionally, Mexican markets are not homogeneous. There are huge regional and class differences, particularly pronounced in urban and agricultural areas. However, Mexico is experiencing a growing middle class.

Mexico is currently reaching to world investment and commerce as never before and, as a result, many multinational companies and franchises are entering Mexico. Nevertheless, Mexico, like the rest of Latin America, differs from the U.S. in that it is a country where small business predominates and production rates and schedules are not always geared to the mass production style of the United States and other highly industrialized countries. Mexico's population of 85 million is growing 1.9 percent a year and this results in poverty and overcrowding. The poorest Mexicans are involved in agriculture (25 percent of the workforce) and produce less than 10 percent of the country's GNP, even with recent radical reform in land ownership rules. It will take decades for real income to reach the level of the poorest Western European countries.

Reduction in the urban birth rate through increased education and job opportunities for all citizens is needed. Education is also still a weak point, but Salinas pledged to attend to it in the remainder of his six-year term. However, as a result of Salinas' progress, many observers on the international scene feel that Mexico's economic and social outlook for the immediate future may be better than it has been for many decades.

Chapter 3

Facts and Figures

Mexico's formal name is The United States of Mexico. It is divided into 31 states and the Federal District (Mexico City) is referred to by its initials, D.F. (*Distrito Federal*). Mexico is a Federal Republic in which some 50 Indian languages are still spoken in addition to Spanish.

Mexico's currency is the peso, and is expressed in writing with the U.S. dollar sign ($). The country received $131 million in U.S. aid in 1991, $32 million in grants (reverse grants, returns, payments) and $98 million (U.S.) in net credits. The U.S. Ambassador to Mexico is currently John Negroponte and the Mexican Ambassador to the U.S. is Gustavo Petricioli.

The country's economy is one-twentieth the size of the U.S. budget. Mexico spends much of its budget on public welfare in order to deal with its social problems including unemployment and unequal distribution of wealth.

POLITICAL ORGANIZATION

The head of the Mexican government is President Carlos Salinas de Gortari (PRI party), elected by universal adult suffrage (age 18 and older). Candidates for the presidency representing the PRI party are chosen by the outgoing president who is limited to only one six-year term, called a *sexenio*. Although there are popular elections and candidates from more than one party in each presidential election, no president other than the candidate from the PRI has won a presidential election since the end of the revolution when revolutionary general Alvaro Obregón took power. The result is that Mexico, in effect, has a one-party system and the president has vast powers in comparison to the two-party system of the United States with its attending system of checks and balances.

There are two houses of congress, also elected, 64 senators (two from each state and two from the Federal District), each with a six-year term. For the 300 electoral districts, there are 500 deputies, elected for three-year terms. (In each election, 300 of the seats in the lower chamber are awarded on a first-past-the-post basis. The other 200 seats are distributed on a proportional representation basis to parties obtaining a national vote of at least 1.5 percent.) As of this writing, the last general elections were held in July 1988.

The country's political parties include the Independent Revolutionary Party (PRI), 60/260, the National Democratic Front (FDN), 4/139, and the National Action Party (PAN), 0/101. The Mexican Democratic Party (PDM) and the Workers' Revolutionary Party (PRT) currently have no representation in the federal government. The main labor organization is the Confederation of Mexican Workers (CTM).

The main employers' organizations are the National Chamber of Processing Industries (CANACINTRA) and the Confederation of Industrial Chambers (CONCAMIN).

POPULATION STATISTICS

Mexico's population is about 80 million (85,090,000 in 1990 and projected to be 99,604,000 in 2000). Mexico boasts of having three of the world's largest cities.

	Population 1990 (est. 2000)	Density 1989 (pop. per sq mi)
Mexico City	20,207,000 (27,872,000)	37,314
Guadalajara	3,262,000 (4,451,000)	40,364
Monterrey	2,837,000 (3,974,000)	35,448

Source: *Geography on File* (1991) NY: Facts on File

The population's density is 43 per square kilometer; infant mortality from 1980 to 1985 is 49.9 per thousand; life expectancy at birth is 65.7; and literacy in 1988 was 84 percent (World Fact Book). The population is 15 percent white (descendents of the Spaniards), 60 percent mestizo (mixed Spanish and Indian), and 25 percent pure Indian (Maya, Aztec, and others). Table 1 further elaborates on Mexico's population.

GEOGRAPHY

Mexico is a large country, covering 756,066 sq miles. Its boundaries cover 8,850 miles: 1,942 miles border the United States; 161 miles border Belize; 598 miles border Guatemala. Its coastline includes the Gulf of Mexico and the Caribbean Sea (1,708 miles), and the Pacific Ocean (4,441 miles).

Mexico's highest point is Orizaba Peak (Citlaltepetl Volcano); at 18,406 feet it is the third highest mountain in the world. The second highest mountain, Ixtacihuatl, is in Toluca at 14,636 feet. Mexico's lowest point is Lake Salada, 26 feet below sea level. Only 12 percent of the land is arable: 1 percent permanent crops; 39 percent meadows and pastures, 24 percent forest and woodland, and 24 percent other. Two-thirds of the country is mountainous and these mountains tend to perpetuate regionalism. Access to many regions is very difficult and these areas remain economically undeveloped and culturally isolated.

The heartland of Mexico is volcanic. Most of the large cities and the densest rural population are located in basins and valleys. Two active volcanos exist in Mexico, Colima, which erupted in 1991, and El Chichon, which erupted in 1983.

Mexico has a number of waterfalls. El Salto is the highest with a 218-foot elevation. Mexico also has desert land. The Chihuahan Desert covers 140,000 square miles from Texas and New Mexico/Arizona through Mexico.

NATURAL RESOURCES

Mexico produces and exports a variety of agricultural products, including corn, rice, wheat, and beans. Commercial crops include

TABLE 1. Mexican States, Capitals, Area, and Population
(1986 estimate)

State	Capital	Area (sq mi/km)		Population
Aguascalientes	Aguascalientes	2,112	5,471	647,000
Baja California Norte	Mexacali	26,997	69,921	1,348,500
Baja California Sur	La Paz	28,369	73,475	291,000
Campeche	Campeche	19,619	50,812	553,000
Chiapas	Tuxtla Gutierrez	28,653	74,211	2,435,300
Chihuahua	Chihuahua	94,571	244,938	2,206,000
Coahuila	Saltillo	57,908	149,982	1,840,900
Colima	Colima	2,004	5,191	405,500
Durango	Durango	47,560	124,181	1,347,100
Guanajuato	Guanajuato	11,773	30,491	3,404,400
Guerrero	Chilpancingo	24,819	64,281	2,469,500
Hidalgo	Pachuca	8,036	20,813	1,771,300
Jalisco	Guadalajara	31,211	80,836	5,049,700
México	Toluca	8,245	21,355	10,650,300
Michoacán	Morelia	23,138	59,928	3,281,900
Morelos	Cuernavaca	1,911	4,950	1,194,200
Nayarit	Tepic	10,417	26,979	824,200
Nuevo León	Monterrey	25,067	64,924	3,032,400
Oaxaca	Oaxaca	36,275	93,952	2,609,500
Puebla	Puebla	13,090	33,902	3,923,300
Querétaro	Queretaro	4,420	11,449	905,900
Quintana Roo	Chetumal	19,387	50,212	351,600
San Luis Potosi	San Luis Potosi	24,351	63,068	1,951,100
Sinaloa	Culiacan	22,521	58,328	2,254,500
Sonora	Hermosillo	70,291	182,052	1,743,700
Tabasco	Villahermosa	9,756	25,267	1,252,600
Tamaulipas	Cuidad Victoria	30,650	79,384	2,207,800
Tlaxcala	Tlaxcala	1,551	4,016	643,900
Veracruz	Jalapa	27,683	71,699	2,207,800
Yucatán	Mérida	14,827	38,402	1,254,000
Zacatecas	Zacatecas	28,283	73,252	1,235,200
Federal District: Distrito Federal		571	1,479	10,051,500
TOTAL		756,066	1,958,201	79,579,900

Source: *Geography on File* (1991) NY: Facts on File

coffee, from the South (Mexico is the world's fifth largest producer), sugar, cottonseed, copper, cotton, and tobacco and bananas (from the Yucatán and Acapulco).

Forestry is important in the Yucatán and central region of the country. Additionally, Mexico is an important producer of livestock and has a large fishing industry (primarily in the Gulf).

Agriculture is heaviest on the central plains. Agriculture is about one-sixth of Mexico's economy and 22 percent of the world's agricultural production is from Mexico. The daily calorie supply is 2,600, or more calories per capita per day than the world's average (quite similar to the U.S.'s calorie production). Government irrigation projects in the 1960s dramatically improved Mexico's agricultural output (*Geography on File*).

Irrigation has played a major role in Mexican economic history. The Morelos Dam on the Colorado River at the head of the Gulf of California converted the desert land in the Mexicali Valley into an important agricultural area, primarily dedicated to cotton farming. In the north, land reclamation through irrigation projects, particularly in areas close to the U.S. border and the Rio Grande, has lead to agricultural development in this previously barren area.

The soils in Central Mexico consist of rich volcanic ash and offer a long growing season, making the Bajio the most productive agricultural zone in Central Mexico. Along the Coast, the lowlands are fertile but hot and marshy. Insect infestation during Mexico's early years was so intense that the port of Veracruz was known as the "City of Death."

In the South Pacific region of Guerrero, Oaxaca, and Chiapas, Colima is, perhaps, the most isolated part of Mexico. Because of the plateau of Central Mexico, this region is cut off from the rest of the country and it is most like the rest of Central America.

Minerals are an important part of the Mexican economy. Mining, construction, and railways were nationalized and supported by the Díaz government. Currently, Mexico is the world's largest producer of silver and is a leader in gold production (see Figure 1), copper, lead and zinc.

Mexico also produces antimony, graphite, sulfur, mercury, and large quantities of iron ore, cadmium, tungsten, manganese, arsenic, and other minerals. Coal is produced in abundance, as is oil and natural gas.

MINING

Tungsten	far northwest
Uranium	northwest, northeast
Copper	north central
Iron	northwest coastal
Gold	west coastal (central)
Zinc	west coastal (central)
Silver	southwest coastal
Lead	east coastal (north central)
Natural Gas	south
Oil	central east, south
Coal	northwest, southwest coastal

Source: *Geography on File* and *Environmental Data Report* (1989)

The petroleum industry is an extremely important part of the national economy (See Figure 2). President Lázaro Cárdenas' decision to nationalize the oil industry on March 18, 1938, was regarded as a major affirmation of national sovereignty and a model for the rest of Latin America. Yet oil had been marketed by Mexico since it was first discovered in 1901. Production was soon expanded by U.S. and British companies who went so far as to finance an army to oppose the central government. The oil issue was troublesome for another two decades until 1937 when President Cárdenas' Mexican oil workers union (STPRM) went on strike. The oil companies protested, and Cárdenas ordered the immediate nationalization of the assets of the 17 British and U.S. companies. While the sudden nationalization decision brought an economic slump–a boycott of Mexican oil products by U.S. companies, and a break in diplomatic relations with the British–it was, in political terms, a major success.

Mexican oil production, export, and earnings from 1977 through 1987 are illustrated in Table 2.

FIGURE 1. Gold Production 1975-1989

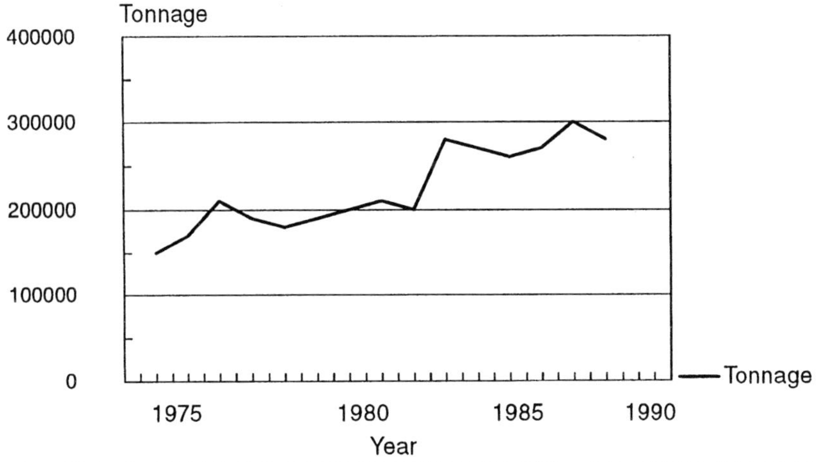

Source: Bureau of Mines, U.S. Department of the Interior

MANUFACTURING

Manufacturing, as a significant contributor to the economy, is a more recent development in Mexico. Textiles developed during the colonial period and the industry itself remained relatively primitive until it was modernized by Lucas Alamán in 1830 (with the creation of a national credit bank to promote industrial and agricultural development). Consumer goods–food processing (vegetable oils, wheat flour), footwear, apparel manufacturing (cotton yarn)–all made great strides during the Porfirio Díaz years (1876-1911).

Additionally, the Mexican government supported heavy industry during the Díaz years (chemicals, cement, iron and steel). Now, these products, besides synthetic fibers, plastics, industrial machinery, and automobiles, are very important to the Mexican economy. Much of Mexico's automotive and general industrial production is centered in Mexico City, Monterrey, and Guadalajara.

Beverages

Beer has been brewed for as long as human habitation has existed in Mexico. In modern times, beer is not considered to be really intoxicating since the alcohol content is under 5 percent by volume.

FIGURE 2. Crude Oil Production 1960-1990

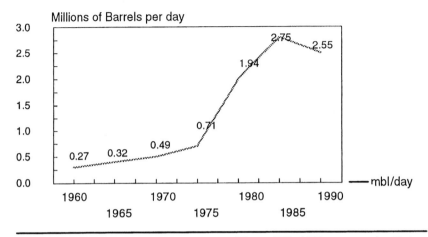

Source: Composite from *Geography on File* and World Resources Institute.

Historically, Mexico was the home of the first commercial New World brewery. Later in the 1890s, the Europeans brought over lager-pilsner brewing technologies from Germany and Austria.

Today, three breweries produce most of Mexico's commercial beer: Cuauhtemoc, whose brands include: Chihuahua, Bohemia, Tecate, Carta Blanca, and Indio; Modelo, whose brands include: Corona, Conmemorativa, Oscura, Sol, and Superior; and Moctezuma, whose brands include: Dos Equis, Tres Equis, Indio Esuvra, Hussong's, and Noche Buena.

INTERNATIONAL TRADE

Mexico's principal imports are chemicals, machinery, appliances, and transportation equipment. Foreigners contemplating doing business in Mexico should keep in mind that Mexican markets are not homogenous since there are huge regional and class differences in consumption. U.S. products are typically regarded as high quality, but U.S. businesses which used to take advantage of

TABLE 2. Mexican Oil Production, Exports and Export Earnings: 1977-1987

Year	Crude Production (000bpd)	Crude Exports (000bpd)	Total Hydrocarbon Exports ($ million)	% of Total Exports
1977	981	202	1018.7	21.9
1978	1209	365	1837.2	30.3
1979	1461	533	3986.5	44.7
1980	1936	828	10401.9	68.0
1981	2312	1098	14574.0	75.0
1982	2746	1492	16594.5	79.0
1983	2665	1537	16164.9	74.9
1984	2685	1525	16601.3	68.0
1985	2630	1438	14606.0	69.0
1986	2428	1290	6132.0	38.9
1987	2604	1237	4211.1	40.6

Source: "Economic Trends Report," U.S. Embassy, Mexico City, Feb. 1987, January to June.

this perception can do so no longer, as a result of stepped-up international competition.

Joint ventures are the most common form of international trade. These are often contracted with companies already doing business in Mexico. As trade barrier protection is weakened, Mexican companies are seeking foreign investment in order to take advantage of economies of scale and make them more competitive globally. These local companies are successful since they know the distribution networks, native culture, and local production facilities.

The U.S. has invested $25 billion in Mexico and tends to hire local management and then leave the business to run itself. One third of the Japanese companies are managed by Japanese nationals. In the near future increased investment is expected from Australia, Spain, Portugal, and Germany.

MAQUILADORA

Maquila or Maquiladora is a nickname for the Border Industrialization Program (PIF) established in 1965. Often referred to as an industry in itself, this program allows U.S. companies to assemble products in low-wage Mexico for reexport to the U.S. Maquilas are required to reexport a majority of their products; in other words, duty-free imports of machines and equipment are used for manufacturing. Components are allowed for assembly as long as at least 80 percent of the plant's output goes for export. This permits 100 percent foreign ownership of plants in Mexico. The U.S. charges duty only on value added to American-made components by assembly work in Mexico. With the removal of duty, Maquilas can become finished product facilities.

The name, Maquila, makes reference to a time when Mexican farmers carted grain to millers for processing (*maquilar*, meaning to manufacture or process) while maintaining ownership of the finished product. This program, started in the 1960s, languished until the 1980s when peso devaluation and a crisis in the American auto industry made the lower Mexican wage rates a competitive factor.

Maquiladoras became an important source of jobs in the 1980s. While the Mexican economy declined by 4 percent in 1986, the number of Maquilas rose by 25 percent and employed 268,400 workers. To make the illustration clearer, the workforce size for Maquiladoras jumped from 119,546 in 1980 to 452,399 in 1991.

Maquilas rival oil and tourism for their total impact on the national economy of Mexico. Over time these companies have changed from simple assembly work to full-scale (automated) manufacturing operations.

Such operations have been successful in attracting Japanese industry. In fact, Japanese presence more than doubled (from 19 to 50 different companies) from 1985 to 1989 in the automotive and electronics industries. More of this is expected as NAFTA is put into effect.

The Free Trade Agreement may give the U.S. and Canada access to Mexico's 85 million consumers and their demand for foreign products, however, some experts speculate that the Maquiladora program may become extinct. The Maquila's existence is due to the trade barriers. However, NAFTA may provide a stronger integration with the Mexican economy and a cost advantage even if labor rates double.

Many small- to medium-sized companies followed larger ones

(particularly suppliers) into Mexico. Big companies want suppliers within a 24 hour radius for just-in-time inventory. The trend is toward self-contained factories and automation and the industries most involved in the program include auto parts, electronics, and clothing, as well as jewelry and medical instrument production. Service industries are involved in Maquilas, as well, from a branch of a San Diego hospital (Baja) to labor intensive nursing homes and health care businesses.

It is important to note that there are some drawbacks to the Maquiladora program. Turnover of local personnel has always been high, as workers may cross the border for higher wages. Additionally, criticism has come from American labor unions, environmentalists, and human rights activists. U.S. business must remember that the cost of setting up a Maquiladora include red tape, labor, infrastructure issues, and distribution. There is a lot of paperwork involved each time materials are sent to Mexico or brought out as finished products.

Lower productivity and higher turnover require companies to employ a larger number of workers. Additionally, one must offset incentives to wage packages (for example, improved housing, clothing allowances, food discounts), and labor laws. Mexican labor laws are also quite different from laws in the U.S. For example, employers must pay a month's salary (or more) to laid off workers, and any changes in staffing are very expensive.

Mexico's infrastructure is underdeveloped and a good deal of money is needed for improvements. There is movement of businesses to the interior of the country (20 percent of the plants are there now), but there are electricity, sewer, water, and communications hookup problems limiting rapid expansion. In addition, reliable distributors are not easy to find. Many are undercapitalized and it is important that U.S. businesses seeking to enter Mexico check their financial information and references and visit their offices to see their distribution capacity for themselves. It is also important to become familiar with banks and local companies in order to check references.

Other problems include sweatshop working conditions, substandard worker housing, the use of child labor, pollution, and waste disposal problems (it costs more for pollution controls and to upgrade deficiencies). Additionally, Mexican traditionalists differ with social changes brought about by a heavy population of women participating in the program. Domestic culture, urban services, consumption, and entertainment opportunities designed especially for a female market, all challenge traditional male-female roles.

Consumers have and are expected to continue to benefit from the Maquiladora program. The cost of traded goods tends to be low and the variety of goods traded is expected to increase (Table 3). U.S. producers benefit from a broader market for their goods and services and U.S. labor benefits from a lower level of immigration. Border towns have particularly benefited from this program. Over 50 percent of the wages earned on the Mexican side have been spent on the U.S. side. Tourism has also made gains; Mexican tourist dollars account for a good deal of U.S. border town municipal government revenues in the form of sales tax.

MAQUILA LOCATIONS

City(ies)	Workers	Plants
El Paso/Juarez	134,838	321
San Diego/Tijuana	65,255	523
Brownsville/Matamoros	38,268	94
McAllen/Reynosa	30,000	82
Chihuahua (interior)	29,229	61
Nogales/Nogales	21,084	80
Laredo/Nuevo Laredo	21,000	93
Calexico/Mexicali	20,732	158
Monterrey (interior)	17,106	75
Del Río/Ciudad Acuña	14,151	44
other	60,736	394

Source: *Twin Plant News*, El Paso, TX, 1991

OTHER INDUSTRIES

Tourism is also a major industry in Mexico. Eighty percent of this industry is from the U.S. In an average Mexico City daily

TABLE 3. Maquiladora Exports
(in $ million)

Industry	1985	1986	1987	1988	1989
Electronics	2,400.0	2,652.0	3,157.0	4,481.0	5,577.0
Transport Equipmt	1,438.8	1,621.8	2,086.2	2,549.8	3,376.8
General Mfg.	335.5	449.9	681.1	1,066.7	1,367.0
Furniture	110.3	145.5	256.2	414.7	572.7
Textiles	376.6	380.4	409.5	487.9	567.8
Toys	164.8	134.9	152.0	283.5	334.8
Services	75.3	82.6	110.7	112.0	203.3
Tools	61.0	73.0	115.6	168.5	183.6
Other	131.2	105.8	136.7	581.6	287.0
TOTAL	5,093.3	5,645.9	7,105.0	10,145.7	12,470.0

Source: Bank of Mexico, *Annual Report* 1990

newspaper there is a higher percent of U.S. news than the average issue of *The New York Times* carries on the entire world.

Advertising is another major service industry. The largest agencies are Publicidat Ferrer (the largest), McCann-Erickson (the second largest), Montenagro-Saatchi & Saatchi (controlling Iconic, Mexico City), BBDO Worldwide-Dieste Merino, and J. Walter Thompson.

LABOR

Mexico has some of the strongest labor laws in the world and ignorance of these laws is no excuse for noncompliance. After a 30-day trial period, workers are regarded as permanent and are virtually impossible to get rid of. Dismissals require the employer to specify reasons and severe penalties are enforced if this process is not properly carried out. It is important to have a qualified Mexican attorney when dealing with such matters.

The labor movement is very important in Mexico's history. The Confederation of Mexican Workers (*Confederacion de Trabajadores Mexicanos*/CTM) is the country's largest union. It was founded in 1936 and is closely aligned with the Independent Revo-

MEXICO'S MAJOR INDUSTRIES

INDUSTRY	TOTAL	COMMENTS
Auto parts and accessories	2.9 billion	Among the last private employer. Plans for expansion.
Electrical, electronics, telecommunications equipment	682.4 million (telecom alone)	11% growth expected (1992). Telephone system recently privatized. Overhaul or electricity generating sector expected.
Apparel manufacturing	(not available)	Long-protected. Needs technology investment.
Mining	(not available)	Eased government restrictions.
Building Materials	(not available)	Infrastructure improvements and increased demand. Restrictions to U.S. wood imports recently lifted.
Franchises	(not available)	New law on technology transfer.
Oil and Gas	1.1 billion	Expected +10% in 1992. No change expected in foreign ownership rules. U.S. sale of related equipment and services expected to grow.
Environmental cleanup services	(not available)	Mexico City, maquiladora regions.
Computers and peripherals	695.8 million	Expected 20% growth, greater specialization, increased imports of more sophisticated equipment.
Industrial chemicals	840 million	Growth 10%. Seeking foreign investment.

Source: International Business Research, *Market Estimates*, U.S. Department of Commerce

lutionary Party (It is one of the three main sectors of the party which includes the CNC, the peasants' representative, and the CNOP, the public employees', professionals', and military representative.)

President Cárdenas formed the CTM in order to overcome corruption existing in the older union, the Confederation of Mexican Workers (CROM). Fidel Velázquez is the most prominent leader of the union. One of the "five little wolves"–a group of officials that controlled the CTM shortly after its foundation–Valázquez became the undisputed leader in 1941. An anti-communist, he forged close ties with George Meany's American Federation of Labor (AFL) and developed a powerful political machine at home.

At government request, the CTM imposed wage restraint and quelled outbreaks of rank-and-file radicalism. Under Lopez Portillo, Velazquez accepted wage increases that were below the rate of inflation and in return got control of the state housing fund. A workers' bank was established and the government persecuted anti-Velázquez independent unions. Válazquez has served eight terms and is presently serving his ninth (elected in 1986 at 86 years old) as CTM general secretary.

Each president since Cárdenas has dealt directly with the CTM. Although there is some question as to specific data regarding the strengths of the different labor unions, the CTM claims to have 11,000 affiliated unions with a membership of over seven million.

THE NORTH AMERICAN FREE TRADE AGREEMENT

Throughout Mexican post-revolutionary history, international trade agreements have played an instrumental part in Mexico's growth and economic development. The General Agreement on Tariffs and Trade (GATT), was the point from which most free trade plans have emerged. The European Community (EC) plans have been progressing and the U.S.-Canadian Free Trade Agreement went into effect in 1989.

The North American Free Trade Agreement (NAFTA) is the Western Hemisphere's answer to European and Australasian discussions. This trilateral plan has gathered popularity as a result of the "silent integration" between Mexican and American economies (Weintraub, 1984).

During the past decade, Mexico has moved from one of the most protectionist to one of the most liberal trade organizations in the world. President Lopez Portillo (1976-1982) rejected the GATT because he feared U.S. domination of oil. After the collapse of oil prices and the debt crisis of 1982, President de la Madrid (1982-1988) began to liberalize the trade process and joined GATT. President Salinas de Gortari (1988) extended his predecessor's policies and has now successfully established the signing of a free trade agreement between Mexico, the United States, and Canada. This plan is expected to rival the European Economic Community system in terms of population and output.

The population of the North American market would be 30 million larger than the EC (360 million vs. 326 million) and would produce more than $6 trillion a year in goods and services (compared with the EC's approximately $4.5 trillion). In fact, NAFTA should create the world's largest market; larger than the EC in population while similar in combined output.

Once settled, NAFTA would cover almost every aspect of trade between the U.S., Mexico, and Canada. It will remove all significant barriers to trade and establish guidelines and rules for investment and intellectual property rights (a weakness right now).

Recent negotiations addressed phaseout periods for specific products and supported nontariff barriers to trade. Additionally, these talks addressed removing barriers to the free flow of investment (e.g., equity or management control restrictions), and services. (Currently, there are no international rules governing services.) Then, in turn, customs issues will also be addressed.

Overall, the impact of the trade agreement on the U.S. may not be dramatic in all sectors. New markets will lower U.S. prices. For example, demand for soybeans should grow, but the sugar beet market will hurt some sectors of the U.S. and Canadian agricultural economies as will vegetables, citrus fruits, and lumber.

Technological and capital intensive industries should benefit greatly (optical goods, machinery and equipment, chemicals, plastics, iron and steel) as well as auto production. Additionally, the U.S. could benefit from trade finance, corporate finance, and retail banking. Opposition from U.S. labor was responded to with promises of a long transition period, retraining programs, and safeguards to allow the U.S. to forestall or retaliate against sharp increases in imports.

The economy of Mexico has improved considerably in the past few years. Inflation in 1990 was 27 percent, while in 1987 it was 170 percent. Government wage and price controls appear to be working and the government deficit dropped from 16 percent gross domestic product to 6.3 percent from 1986 to 1989. Additionally, in anticipation of the free trade agreement, Mexico lowered tariffs in 1992 10 to 11 percent on average and the maximum tariffs have dropped from 100 percent in the early 1980s to 20 percent today.

While these numerous government policies have helped considerably, Mexico still faces some difficulty in getting Mexicans to invest in their country. In order to encourage domestic investment, the banks pay a real interest rate of 35 percent. Still, investments in foreign markets are estimated as high as $80 billion.

NAFTA is expected to reassure skittish investors that Mexico will not reduce free-market trends toward reducing protectionism and government involvement in the economy. It is expected to accelerate migration of manufacturing jobs to Mexico, and the U.S. will benefit as well. Many believe that a better use of resources will result, especially in light of the competitive challenge of the EC, Eastern Europe, and Japan. Also, it has been estimated that an additional 25,000 new jobs will be created in the U.S. for each $1 billion of increased U.S.-Mexican trade.

NAFTA is expected to bring about a free trade zone and eliminate most tariff barriers and increase investment flows. In all three countries, there are producers that will be hurt by freer trade among the three nations. Overall, though, most economists believe that the major NAFTA member nations will experience gains in employment, wages, per capita income, and living standards. Countries that have been the United State's main trading partners are those that will experience some losses.

STOCK MARKET

There has been a lot of growth in the activity of the Mexican stock market in recent years. Market capitalization and the generation of capital through sale of stock has accelerated beyond imagination. Global enthusiasm has been tremendous. In 1989 the Mexican stock market capitalization in U.S. dollars was $22.6 billion.

Since 1989 Mexican stocks outpaced U.S. stock gains which were, themselves, strong, just as they outpaced European and Japanese stocks. Luis Guillermo Medina, the Deputy Director of Communications for the Mexican Stock Exchange, reported that, in 1989, Mexico's stock market registered a 68 percent return on the dollar.

Mexico's first stock exchange opened in 1894 to serve the market for stocks in mining banks. The market remained relatively quiet until 1975, when the president decreed the creation of treasury bills. Once federal funds were part of the country's exchange, and the market became a provider of capital for both public and private sectors, the market took off. About 100 major businesses rely on the market as a source of expansion project financing. It also serves as a source to small- and mid-sized banks for short-term financing and provides a means for federal financing.

The exchange is located in Mexico City. All in all, almost 20 different instruments are available through the market for financing and investment. Because of the debt crisis and slowdown in bank lending to Mexico, the country needed new sources of commercial financing. These factors served to undervalue Mexican stock and make it a good bargain from the perspective of the international finance community at the same time that security laws were revised in the late 1970s.

While growth has been phenomenal, the market still plays a relatively minor role in the national economy. Compared to the New York Stock Exchange, the Mexican Exchange is relatively small. The Mexican business structure is dominated by owner-operators who maintain tight control over their majority shares.

Mexico was a leader in offering national funds. It was the first Latin American source in 1987 and during the next five years, 10 more country funds have been formed. Internationally, 29 have opened from October 1988 through March 1990, only 17 of which are in Europe. Foreign capital supports prices and gives confidence in Mexican investors and stability to the market.

Impulsora del Fondoa Mexico is listed on stock exchanges in New York, London, and Stuttgart. PEMEX, the state oil company, issued $722 million in internal bonds since 1989. Telmex, newly privatized, sold $2 billion in shares.

More efficient markets will create more wealth and more investment. As a result a new wave of foreign investors and the return of flight capital is expected. This will further reinforce locals in keeping their money at home.

A PICTURE OF THE MARKET
1980-88

Indicator of Performance	1980	1984	1988
Number of companies listed	259	160	203
Market capitalization (in billion $ U.S.)	13.0	2.2	13.8
Stock Market Index (1980=100)	100	282	14,722
Consumer Price Index (80=100)	100	619	9,904

Source: International Finance Corporation, *Emerging Stockmarkets Factbook*, 1990, Washington, DC.

TRANSPORTATION

Prior to the conquest, transport was generally done on human back. The rich were carried in litters. There is evidence that canoes made from tree trunks were used on navigable rivers and lakes and were used to carry both trade and people. The Spaniards brought horses, mules, and burros, but the natives continued to perform manual labor. Even today, pack trains and mules or burros still work in rural areas and *arrieros*, or animal drivers, rely on their *mesones* (stopping places or shelters) for both themselves and their animals.

Given the proper attitude, though, visitors to Mexico should find the transportation quite satisfactory to meet their needs. There are some obstacles for international rail transport. It is not unusual for border delays of a day or more. Sometimes paperwork gets lost. One can also expect to lose some time with inspections (an entire train can be held up if a container is suspect). Finally, the infrastructure is sometimes poor, there is a shortage of engines, and operating practices are sometimes inadequate by U.S. standards. However, there is a growing degree of cooperation between U.S. and Mexican railroads and this has significantly simplified rail transport. NAFTA is expected to dramatically improve business for the railroads.

However, time is not the same in Mexico as it is in Western Europe and public transportation, while different, can be relied upon, as the visitor in Juan José Arreola's short story, "The Switchman" found out. In the story, a stranger, while waiting at a railroad station, meets an old switchman and inquires about service to the town "T."

> This country is famous for its railways, as you know. Up to now it hasn't been possible to organize them completely, but already great strides have been taken in regard to publishing timetables and issuing tickets. The railroad guides include and link up all the cities in the nation, tickets are issued even for the smallest, most remote villages. The only thing lacking is for the trains to follow the indications contained in the guides and indeed stop at the appointed stations. Citizens hope for progress; in the meantime, they accept irregularities in service and their patriotism prevents them from showing any sign of displeasure.

This classic of Mexican literature should not be taken literally, however, since it is both a satire on transportation (with a view that is almost half a century old already) and is also, more importantly, to be read as the author's symbolic view of the uncertainties of life itself. In that sense it is more a universal story than a truly Mexican one. As a result, modern travelers who have read this important contribution to Mexican literature are cautioned not to take this view of the Mexican railway system too much to heart.

Railroads

Mexico has a long and rich history of railroading. During the Porfirio Díaz years (1876-1911), the government provided tremendous support for the railway industry. In the 1920s a program of public works was underway–under President Plutarco Elías Calles– building many of today's roads.

Train travel is both a matter of economics and personal preference. It is safer and cheaper than the bus (sometimes half the bus fare) but it is slower. Schedules are apt to be a bit more inconvenient than the bus. Major railways include the Nogales to Guadalajara run, Cuidad Juárez to Mexico City, Monterrey to Tampico, Texas to Mexico City, and Mexico City to Veracruz which extends to the end of the Yucatán, Guatemala, and Belize.

The Mexican National Railways (*Ferrocarriles Nacionales de Mexico*) exist alongside the Pacific Railroad Company (*Ferrocarriles del Pacifico*). From the border (Nogales) to Guadalajara takes 26 to 36 hours. From Mexicali, it takes 30 hours to reach Guadalajara, 45 hours to Mexico city (but the trip is several hours faster on the northern run). Mexico has 20,680 kilometers (about 17,000 miles) of railroad (the most in the Caribbean and Central America).

Highways

There are 18,000 miles of paved roads and almost an equal amount of surfaced roads. Roads are generally quite good, however foreign drivers must remember that safety markings are different. Mexican autos still use leaded fuel and octane ratings are a bit lower than U.S. citizens are accustomed to. There are also fewer gas stations per mile of road than U.S. and Canadian residents are used to. Parking can be a problem in the cities, so public bus and train transportation is cheaper and sometimes more convenient.

It is best to avoid driving at night because of differences in road conditions and lighting, as well as to avoid the abundance of trucks, carts, bicyclists, and pedestrians. It is easy to hit potholes, animals, rocks, dead ends, and bridges without warning. Additionally, people in the countryside are not as good at judging the speed of an approaching car.

There are also a number of toll bridges and toll roads in the country along the four basic routes from the U.S. to Mexico. From the western U.S., one would cross the border at either Nogales or El Paso. From the eastern U.S., Nuevo Laredo is the most common border crossing. Eagle Pass, Texas (across the border from Piedras Negras in Coahuila) offers a route to Mexico City which is one of the country's newest and best roads (Route 57)–the weather is pleasant and there are no really huge mountain passes.

Trucking is very important to the country's economy. The government is only in its early stages of building a system of divided, limited-access highways so that truck and car traffic is easy for both vehicles involved. Mufflers and pollution control systems are generally not required of trucks.

Air Travel

Mexico has two national air carriers, Mexicana, Latin America's largest air carrier which originated in 1921, and AeroMexico, formerly a government-owned airline (bankrupt in 1988), now privatized, and sold to Aerovias de Mexico. Air transport reaches the most remote parts of the country. Small local lines carry *chicle* (chewing gum) and other freight even into Chiapas and the Yucatán.

Final Note

Nearly all goods shipped between the U.S. and Mexico are moved by truck or rail. In anticipation of the signing of the NAFTA, United States carriers began preparing to enter the Mexican market. One development already underway is a system of uniform operating procedures. The Finance Ministry expects confusion stemming from different procedures in different parts of Mexico to be eliminated. The prosecution of corrupt customs agents has, also, been stepped up, and both the U.S. and Mexico are addressing the insufficient number of border crossings. Rail should help to bypass crowded customs checkpoints and poor road conditions.

ORGANIZATIONS WITH INFORMATION ABOUT BUSINESS IN MEXICO

A number of organizations and agencies provide information about business relations in Mexico. A few are listed below.

Inter-American Commission on Human Rights
Organization of American States
1889 F Street NW
Washington, DC 20006
202/789-6000

This organization was developed to observe and protect human rights in the Americas. It is the consultative organ of the OAS on these issues. It answers inquiries and distributes publications for free.

Inter-American Bar Foundation
1819 H Street NW, Suite 310
Washington, DC 20006
202/293-1455

This organization's goal is the administration of justice for the Western Hemisphere. It publishes material, answers inquiries, and conducts seminars. Most services are free.

Inter-American Development Bank
181 17th Street NW
Washington, DC 20577
101/634-8000

This organization's purpose is social and economic development in Latin America. It provides general reference services, analyzes data, conducts seminars, and permits onsite use of its library. General services are free, seminars and training are available only through preselection.

Inter-American Nuclear Energy Commission
Organization of American States
1889 F Street NW
Washington, DC 20006
101/789-3368/9/70

This organization publishes reports, conducts inquiries, and provides reference services for free. It makes referrals to other information sources.

Museum of Anthropology
Pennsylvania State University
University Park, PA 16802
814/865-3853

This museum covers archaeology and ethnology and holds ceramics from around the world, especially from Mexico, Afghanistan, Polynesia, and the U.S. It answers inquiries and permits onsite use of the collection by the public free of charge.

International Boundary and Water Commission–U.S. and Mexico
4110 Rio Bravo
El Paso, TX 79902
915/541-7300

This organization is responsible for the administration of treaties and other agreements regarding international land and water boundaries. It publishes bulletins with statistical information, answers inquiries, and makes referrals.

Chapter 4

First Impressions

A CASE HISTORY

A visiting businessman from the United States was invited to a dinner party by a Mexican business associate. The invitation said that the party was going to start at seven p.m. The visitor, of course, arrived at seven. His host was very upset and the visitor noticed that his relations with the host were never quite the same after that. The visitor failed to realize that time is relative to each particular culture one encounters.

TIME

Perhaps the most notorious cultural difference between Anglo-Saxon and Latin cultures centers on the value of time. The subject of outrageous stereotypes and not a few jokes, it is true that both cultures traditionally value time in a different way. It is important to realize, however, that this difference is not merely a superficial one, rather it goes to the heart of the way the two cultures view life. This difference has been well captured by Andrew Gonzalez writing in *Psychology Today* where he comments that Latins have both, "strong present and past perspectives, they see us as obsessed with working, efficiently and rationally, delaying gratification and planning for what will be" (in "Time in Perspective," *Psychology Today*, March 1985, p. 21).

The predominance of rationality may be seen in the U.S. tendency to divide the working day into neat compartments with conscious or subconscious goals for each segment of the daily schedule. Not only are long-range work goals set into schedules, but daily, even routine activities are seen as immutable parts of an overall pattern.

Mexicans tend to be more flexible in their concept of time. This is seen as part of a global perspective as defined by Edward Hall, one of the pioneers of intercultural study, in his book, *Hidden Differences*. In this work Hall divides the world into monochronic and polychronic cultures. As we might expect, Mexican culture turns up on the polychronic end of this scale. Time is more relative in Mexico than in the U.S., and people are generally capable of accomplishing more than one task at a time.

Hall states that in a monochronic culture, such as that found in the United States, there is generally a five- to ten-minute tolerance for lateness before a meeting will be considered cancelled or for which the person arriving late may be considered rude in keeping the other person waiting. In other cultures, including Latin America, there may be up to a half hour or even more tolerance for tardiness.

As a result, there is less sense of rush and pressure in accomplishing personal and business goals in Latin American culture. Indeed, the perceived need to keep up with fast-changing events is more prevalent in U.S. society. We are bombarded with bulletins and items of general news suggesting that we live in a rapidly changing world in which we have to be constantly informed about fast-breaking events.

Although this is also true in urban Mexico, traditional Mexican culture which tends to value constancy, often looks for permanence rather than temporary and fleeting novelty. An example of this is a story of a man living in a rural part of Mexico who was walking down the street while a woman was hawking the latest newspaper. He bought a paper and read it. The very next day he walked down the same street and again found the same woman hawking that day's paper. As he began to walk by the woman without purchasing a paper, the woman asked if he was going to buy another paper and his reply was "Why should I? I already read yesterday's paper."

International businesspeople should be cautioned about taking these cultural time differences as absolute, however, since there has been a recent trend for Mexican businesspeople and government officials to adopt a more international concept of time. Still, this may only be the case at the highest levels of international business and policy, and in large urban areas. Nevertheless, it is important for businesspeople from the U.S. to understand that the sense of urgency and pressure, which is so much a part of their culture, may appear radically different in Mexico. As a result, be cautioned not to "get right down to business" upon introduction to Mexican business counterparts. Mexicans feel that U.S. businesspeople are too cold and brusque in their dealings with others and those who are "on the clock," may well fall into this negative stereotype.

GETTING DOWN TO BUSINESS

It is customary for U.S. businesspeople to engage in only a perfunctory amount of small talk for five or ten seconds before getting down to business. Usually this talk is about the weather or sports, and so forth. Mexicans are likely to continue their conversation for a much longer period of time, upwards to an hour or even more. One of the authors once had a meeting with a very high government official from a major Latin American nation in which the official took almost three hours of general, introductory conversation and small talk before he decided that he wanted to get down to business.

U.S. businesspeople who carry their sense of urgency into business conversations in Mexico, either by the coldness of their facial expressions or by repeatedly looking at their watch, can make a very bad impression. They run the risk of leaving Mexicans with the impression that their business is of momentary and negligible importance. Latins, on the other hand, prefer to establish a relationship with their foreign counterparts before they begin to do business with them. Therefore business dealings and meetings often cannot be slotted into neat little slots on a business calendar.

Indeed the mixing of business and pleasure in social events is very common, since the social aspect of business is more important in Mexico than it is in the United States. Mexicans generally want to socialize with their business colleagues from other countries before engaging in business with them.

Americans will find that once a personal relationship has been formed, business dealings become facilitated to a surprising degree.

This is precisely why attention to the social amenities becomes especially important for visiting businesspeople.

CORDIALITY, PRECISION, AND CULTURE

Mexicans appreciate the expression of politeness and cordiality. Americans who are used to a brusker, more efficiency-oriented society should never forget the great importance of saying "hello" and "thank you" as well as the other forms of social courtesy. Though this may seem quite obvious, it is possible to create an unfavorable impression by ignoring the local customs relating to time at social events.

For example, in Mexico it is not considered polite for a guest to arrive at the time specified by an oral or written invitation. If one is invited to arrive at a party at 8:00 p.m. one would be well advised to understand that arrival before 8:30 or even 9:00 is not expected. Hosts will not be expecting their guests at 8:00 sharp and they, themselves, will not be ready to greet them at the beginning of the evening's festivities.

This flexibility in time can also extend to appointments in general. A U.S. businessperson may be told that Mr. X will be in the office and will be happy to meet with him next Tuesday at 2:00 p.m. From an American standpoint Mr. X will be in his office at that time barring some unforseen emergency or a drastic change of plans. The U.S. businessperson expects that what he or she is told will generally be true under ordinary circumstances. What he or she does not realize, however, is that the United States is what cultural relativists have often called an information-specific society while Latin America constitutes an information-nonspecific society. What this means is that information given in the U.S. is generally right on the mark while information in Latin America very often has little to do with reality.

An example might be the case of a U.S. businessman who tried to reach a Mexican official on the phone. He first thought he would be able to reach him in a few moments by simply picking up the telephone and dialing a long-distance number. He dialed that number, but it literally rang busy for months. When he finally did make contact, he realized that the busy signal may have simply meant that the call had not always gone through.

At any rate, when he asked to speak to the Mexican official, he was first told that the official had left his organization. Another time he was told that the official was available only in the evening. On another occasion he was told just the opposite–that the official worked only from 8:30 a.m. to 3 p.m. He left messages and was earnestly assured that the Mexican official would return his call; however, this never happened. After months of calling he finally made contact with a different official, since the official he was trying to contact had actually left the organization.

There were probably a number of cultural time factors at work in this example. Not only was the information given nonspecific (to put it charitably), but the lack of concern for the absolute accuracy on the part of secretaries and the official himself was typically Latin. Schedules, deadlines, and a general sense of urgency with which business is conducted is traditionally radically different in Latin America than it is in the United States.

FATALISM AND A SENSE OF CONTROL

Some historians of culture and social commentators have spoken of fatalism as one of the hallmarks of Hispanic culture, while American culture is marked by a strong sense of belief in the power of an individual to control his/her own destiny as well as the destiny of society at large. Latin fatalism, however, sees the human condition as a product of destiny. The implications that arise from this cultural difference not only affect each individual but they also affect the way in which business is conducted.

U.S. businesspeople typically feel it is entirely in their power to adhere to rigid production schedules. Many U.S. businesspeople working in a Hispanic environment commented that the Latin businessperson may be more likely to chalk up delays and upsets in schedules as a product of destiny expressing an attitude which says in effect, "Well we tried our best but we couldn't meet the deadline. It just wasn't in the cards."

This same attitudinal difference has a bearing on quality control factors. While a U.S. producer will usually adhere to strict quality control in the manufacture of a product, the Latin manager will tend to take a more philosophical attitude toward production. He is more likely to feel that a product, meeting basic specifications, coming off an assembly in an anticipated amount of time is fine. His attitude toward production standards may be much more philosophical than that of his American counterpart. In effect, the statement, "Well, we tried our best, but nobody is always perfect," is fully accepted.

It is equally true, however, that Mexicans are acutely aware of their current need to adhere to international standards in light of the North American Free Trade Agreement and Mexico's greatly increased international trade. Attitudes are changing and increased importance is given to strict quality control. Still it would be a mistake for a U.S. businessperson entering into business agreements in Mexico, or considering moving their production facilities to Mexico, to consider that the adoption of American and/or international methods of quality control to be absolute and immediate.

DEFERENCE

The same may be said of traditional social relations in Mexico. If U.S. citizens tend to be more formal in respect to matters of time, just the opposite is often true in the interpersonal relations between Americans and Mexicans. As noted before, Mexicans are very class conscious. Businesspeople from the U.S. should always introduce themselves and present their business cards and would be well advised to give more than a split second's attention to the information, name, and title given on any business card they receive.

At the same time, professional titles are considered paramount. This can be disconcerting to people from the U.S. since the most commonly used title, *Licenciado*, which refers to any person who has a graduate or professional degree, does not have a strict counterpart in English.

People from the U.S. are notorious for exporting a breezy informality in their business dealings, shaking hands and calling their counterparts in foreign countries by their first name. Though the importance of building a personal relationship as a prelude to doing business can hardly be overstated in Mexico, this relationship cannot be built on the spot and informality and overfamiliarity can be resented by a Mexican. Mexicans, as well as many others, feel that people from the U.S. are too ready to begin a conversation on a first name basis. Additionally, the American propensity for shortening names is seen as very strange, and potentially offensive. A Mexican finds it hard to understand how Americans could be so familiar with one of their presidents that they called him Jimmy Carter instead of James Carter.

Along the same lines, Mexicans find it hard to understand and sympathize with the informality that can exist between an American manager and his or her employees. Reflecting the greater social democracy in U.S. society, employees commonly call their bosses by their first name and, since managers also tend to call employees by their first names, an apparent lack of social distance appears to exist. Nevertheless, Mexicans are quick to point out that this supposed equality is of course nothing but an illusion. Mexicans prefer to keep the lines of authority more clear and an employee will generally refer to his or her boss on a last name basis or by a professional title such as Doctor or *Licenciado*.

PERSONAL SPACE

Students of social communication have noted that the personal space allowable between individuals differs from one culture to another. Depending upon the situation, an average U.S. citizen feels most comfortable anywhere from 18 inches to six feet apart from those with whom they are conversing. Mexicans feel comfortable at a relatively close distance of 18 to 21 inches. Anyone speaking to a Mexican and standing at an American-style distance runs the risk of appearing cold, distant, and uninterested in what is being said.

GREETINGS

There is no single form of greeting and, in Mexico, one can experience a whole series of greetings. Men shake hands as a matter of course and they tend to walk arm in arm, especially when involved in intense conversation or thought. Women who have met on a few different occasions kiss when they meet.

Embraces, however, are not necessarily signs of affection, but rather of reassurance. Handshakes can follow a pattern from a simple handshake to the *abrazo*, a handshake with a couple of hearty coordinated backslaps, to a second handshake and shoulder slap. As in the United States, the quality of the greeting, particularly the embrace, tends to be scrutinized in political circles for evidence of favor.

One must also be careful when greeting superiors. If the superior resists one's enthusiasm, one faces humiliation. On the other hand, a voluntary *abrazo* from one's boss, particularly in public, is to be celebrated.

Corresponding differences exist in other aspects of interpersonal communication. People from the U.S. speaking Spanish should remember that there are two forms of address relating to the pronoun "you," the familiar form which is addressed by the subject pronoun *tú* and the more formal form of address which is addressed by the subject pronoun *usted*. The familiar form of address should be used when the speaker feels that he or she is on a first name basis with the person to whom s/he is speaking. The more formal manner of address should be used when the discussion is on a more traditional, last name basis.

Do not be overly anxious to use the familiar form of address or to begin a conversation with a Mexican business colleague on a first name basis. Caution should also be used in speaking to Mexicans with abbreviated first names such as "Pepe" and "Pancho" unless they are invited to do so or their relationship with the foreign colleague is of sufficient duration for them to use the familiar form of address.

TELEPHONE ETIQUETTE

When speaking over the telephone Mexicans commonly use the expression *bueno* to say hello and *adiós* or *hasta la vista* to say goodbye. Mexicans value courtesy in all social relations, and this also holds true for phone conversations. In asking for information or to speak to a particular person it is wise to ask if "I may be able to speak with Mr X," or the corresponding Spanish form *quisiera* (I would wish or I might wish.) These are preferable to blunt statements such as "Let me speak with Mr. X." or "Put Mr. X on the phone."

Arranging appointments and evaluating a message that says that Mr. X will be asked to call back, requires you to keep in mind the aforementioned difference between information-specific and information-nonspecific societies. Also remember that, in Mexico, formality can be valued over the accuracy of specific statements. Lastly, those concerned with proper business etiquette in Mexico should remember that it is considered impolite to call a businessperson about a business matter in his or her own home. Business matters are taken care of at the office only.

AMERICAN IMPATIENCE

There are many different cultural factors that U.S. businesspeople have to deal with in Mexico, not to mention the very obvious cultural shock that hits almost all visitors to a different culture. It is very possible for visitors to become impatient with what they perceive to be impracticality and inefficiency in the Mexican way of doing things. As a result, they may be tempted to try to tell their Mexican counterparts how business should be conducted. Sensitivity is the key issue here.

Mexicans are quick to perceive and resent a patronizing attitude on the part of visiting foreigners. To that end, Americans doing business in Mexico would be well advised to weigh the impact of their words very carefully.

This sensitivity to Mexican cultural values also extends to the type of words used in a conversation. Recently Lee Iacocca caused a stir while speaking with Japanese businessmen in Japan because he used expressions that one Japanese official considered to be typical of the language of a gangster. Mexicans are also sensitive to the "blunt" expressions that people from the U.S. use as a matter of course, and U.S. visitors should keep this in mind.

Similarly, derogatory comments about Mexicans and their culture, even if mentioned in jest, should be avoided at all costs. Mexicans are extremely nationalistic, and they greatly resent any patronizing reference to them, their country, or their culture. As an example of how easily Mexicans can be offended by such talk, we need only remember how President Carter offended Mexicans with his reference to the quality of the water in Mexico during one of his trips south of the border. During a recent trip to Mexico the authors found that Mexicans still express their disapproval of these statements over a decade after they were made.

When one considers that Mexicans have a more vivid appreciation of history than those in the U.S. and tend to be more nationalistic and protective of the relative value of their national cultures, it becomes very easy to understand why Mexicans may seem touchy about what they perceive as an American lack of respect. One only has to reflect on such realities as the Mexican-American war, in which Mexico lost vast areas of its territories to the United States, and repeated United States' intervention in Latin American politics to realize why Mexicans could or should be sensitive to the United States' real or imaginary lack of respect for them and their traditions.

It is for this reason that U.S. visitors in Mexico should be wary of introducing themselves as Americans or even North Americans. Many Americans do not realize that Mexico is a part of North America and, therefore, a Mexican has just as much right to introduce himself or herself as a North American as a person from the United States does. For a visitor from the U.S. to not be sensitive to this fact suggests that he or she feels that Mexico lacks any real importance in geographic terms.

Likewise, all of the Western Hemisphere is America and even though Mexicans and all Latin Americans realize that in common parlance citizens of the United States refer to themselves as Americans, some Mexicans resent this terminology. They feel that it arrogantly implies that only citizens of the United States really count in the Western Hemisphere. When Americans are reminded of these facts they commonly ask, "Well, then, how should I introduce myself in Mexico?" While most Latins do not, in fact object to an American employing terms such as "North American" or "American," some do, and it is impossible to tell how one's foreign counterpart will react to any such term. As a result, it is better to simply say that you are from the United States, or to use the corresponding adjective to denote an American in Spanish, *Soy estadounidense* (I am from the United States).

COLLOQUIALISMS

Finally U.S. visitors should attempt to become aware of the relative nature of common sayings and expressions of the Hispanic world as they are used in Mexico. When asking to speak to someone or when asking for a piece of information one is often answered by the expression *momentito* literally "just wait one moment." This moment should not always be taken literally since it can mean anything from one minute to never. Likewise Latins are likely to say as guests are leaving a party, *Aquí tienes tu casa* (Your home is here) or its variant *Mi casa es tu casa* (My home is your home). These are ancient forms of Hispanic hospitality that go back centuries and, of course, are not to be taken literally.

There is a story of a businessman from the United States in Latin America who was very unfamiliar with Hispanic customs. One of his customers had just purchased a ten carat diamond ring and was showing it off to the American. The admiring American said that the ring was beautiful and the Latin responded with the expression *Es tuyo* (It's yours). The American took the expression literally and asked for the ring. The Latin, who was so much a product of his culture that he could not refuse the American's request actually gave the ring away. Only later when the U.S. businessman was told by his local colleagues that the expression of generosity was certainly not meant to be taken literally did he return the ring to its original owner.

U.S. pragmatism has little room for such apparently frivolous expressions, yet attention to the fine points of language and personal conduct can have potentially monumental consequences. They definitely present a problem for those from the U.S. doing business overseas since these expressions are not traditionally outlined in either books or courses on international business, nor are such fine points of culture usually given in books on Latin American civilization and history. When it comes to the fine points of language, dictionaries themselves will not solve all the problems that U.S. visitors will face in Mexico. On the contrary, they may present new problems since expressions such as the one just mentioned above should not only to be translated word by word, they must be understood within the culture. Likewise, a dictionary will give many possible translations for a given word, but will not tell what a certain word may mean in a certain context or what particular connotations it may have.

An example of this occurred during the United States negotiations with Panama. The U.S. State Department sent a message to the government of Panama that it was ready to *Discutir el problema del canal*. The word *discutir* looks very much like its English cognate, "discuss" and indeed that is what the dictionary says. The Americans were surprised to find that the Panamanians were offended by the American statement since *discutir* has another connotation meaning "to argue." The Panamanians were offended that the Americans wanted to begin their negotiations with such a hostile stance.

Such problems, both cultural and linguistic, happen all the time, and almost any U.S. citizen who has attempted to do business in Mexico or the rest of Latin American has similar stories of cross-cultural nightmares. Other U.S. citizens, now considering the possibility of doing business in Mexico, can go far in the direction of eliminating such traumas by realizing the need for increased sensitivity and knowledge about the Mexican people. They must take the need to attempt to comprehend cross-cultural differences relating to conduct as well as language very seriously.

Chapter 5

Communications

A CASE HISTORY

A U.S. management consultant working in Mexico made a presentation to a group of Mexican businessmen and women. He expected that his presentation would go extremely well since this same talk had earned him fantastic feedback in the United States. However, after he finished his Mexican audience seemed to look at him with displeasure, even distrust.

"What was the problem?" he asked a Mexican colleague. "Didn't they like my presentation?"

"No. It was great," answered the Mexican. "It wasn't the speech that got them mad–it was the way you distributed the handouts."

"What?" answered the consultant incredulously.

"That's right," said the Mexican. "You pushed them in front of each person. In Mexico you have to hand papers carefully to each person in your audience if you want to make friends and make a good impression. You just can't do it the American way."

The communications process, even for individuals from the same culture, is often fraught with error and misunderstandings. The words we choose and their myriad of meanings, our body language, the way we open a discussion and our small talk, as well as our listening posture and actions, all influence what we hear and what others hear from us. Whether negotiating a contract or composing a sales letter, caution must be taken to ensure that our message is being accurately presented and received.

Considering the additional difficulty of cross-cultural communication, it is a wonder, sometimes, that international trade and business practices even exist. While not offering a prescription or solution to cross-cultural communications, this chapter should shed some light on our similarities and differences.

SOCIAL RELATIONSHIPS

It is difficult to begin a discussion about communications without a brief overview of social relationships. Perhaps the first place to begin, when considering Mexico, is with politeness. Not only do Mexicans tend to be polite to strangers, but they are polite even among themselves. Older people are greeted with respect, even to the extent of kissing a revered senior's hand. When adults meet, their salutations include wishes for health and well-being.

Body signals are also sent in terms of one's stance. As mentioned in the previous chapter, Mexicans tend to stand closer to each other than people from the U.S. It is very important, though, to note the reserve between the sexes. Men and women keep a considerably larger distance from each other than they do with their own sex.

Borrowing is another area in which courtesy rules. Any borrowed object is returned with a gift (one should never expect anything for nothing). If a favor, however slight, is asked of a stranger (even a government official), one must offer something in return for making the request.

The manner in which one deals with time is also a potential source of conflict, in terms of courtesy, on the part of someone from the U.S. It has been suggested that Mexicans have a greater sense of continuity and therefore a greater sense of the past. The past is not dead, rather it joins the present/living as an everyday occurrence. For example, instead of Halloween being celebrated near All Saints Day early in November, (although in recent years the celebration of Halloween has been entering some parts of Mexico), the Day of the Dead (November 2) is celebrated, with partying at gravesides and a sense of communion with the departed.

Mexicans tend to be very conscious of their past, to the extent of speaking of historical events as current issues. They also view the future as predetermined. This fatalism is expressed in a number of ways. Planning is an unnatural behavior. Large, fast profits are valued over long-term expansion of a market. Many workers spend rather than save, and any saving that is done is often for a fiesta, such as a *quinceanera* party (the equivalent of a U.S. sweet sixteen party), or for short-term use rather than put in a bank.

Time is relative in Mexico. As we have noted, punctuality in one's social life is not particularly important. While appearances are also a very important part of courtesy. The poor spend elaborately, even going into debt, for fiestas, weddings, birthday parties, and funerals. Presents express both the wealth of the donor and also the importance of the recipient. Men wrestle for the privilege of picking up the check in a restaurant (and the U.S. "Dutch treat" or split bill is often considered offensive). The powerful keep an entourage of aids and bodyguards who whisper messages and open the way through traffic bottlenecks. *Machismo* can be measured by the number of dependents one has.

A great deal of symbolism is attached to a Mexican inviting a stranger into his/her home. Mexicans tend to be very private about their home life and naturally cautious about people outside the extended family. While entertainment away from the home is a regular occurrence for men in business, being invited to another's home is considered an attempt at forming an emotional bond, becoming a *cuate*, or twin. Openness of this sort suggests a willingness to confide and trust and must not be taken lightly; home-based hospitality is among the greatest of compliments.

A NATIONAL PERSONALITY

The Mexican "personality" needs to be taken into account when one attempts communications. Since the goal of any successful message is to reach its audience, a firm understanding of the audience is a must. People from the U.S. tend to think of Mexicans as friendly and sympathetic and feel a genuine affinity for the people. In a public opinion survey conducted by Gallup in 1986, people in the U.S. were asked how they viewed various world cultures and Mexico was ranked among the top. The only foreign country U.S. travelers visited more often was Canada and so, from direct experience, they reported perceptions of Mexico as a "stable, reliable, and friendly" neighbor.

Mexicans, though, tend to see the U.S. a bit differently. The national character is one of long memory. Mexicans have a far more intense sense of history than U.S. citizens do and they remember and fear United States intervention.

Likewise, the U.S. presence in Mexico can, at times, seem overwhelming and Mexicans often view institutions in a different way. While people in the U.S. see little coordination and unity in leisure, business, journalistic/world press, and government matters, many Mexicans view the presence of these institutions as a controlling force on the national economy, with the relationship between U.S. business interests and U.S. federal government "officialdom" as incestuous. While U.S. residents do not tend to see their press as anything close to a unified entity, they must remember that in Mexico, journalists are more closely allied with the government.

Simply put, U.S. business in Mexico has grown to almost 25 times its size in 1950, and while the U.S. share of foreign investment in Mexico has declined since 1950, about one-quarter of Mexico's external debt is to the U.S. The U.S.' official (government) presence is greater in Mexico than in any other country.

Additionally, U.S. pensioner retirees, businesspersons, students, researchers, and consultants make a visible presence in Mexico. As of 1990 the State Department register showed over 275,000 U.S. citizens residing in Mexico, most likely fewer than are actually there. Over 100,000 reportedly live in Mexico City, alone.

While presence does not necessarily mean influence, Mexicans find the two harder to separate than U.S. citizens. Slightly over half of all movies shown in Mexico are from the U.S., despite Mexico's historically thriving film industry. U.S. television has a big influence on Mexican TV and rock music. U.S. hamburgers, jeans, and other consumer products have a tremendous influence on everyday Mexican life as well as the values of the young.

Businesspeople who spend a considerable amount of time in Mexico learn that it is necessary to be discreet: one should not even think about lobbying for trade, tax, or investment policies, but should leave those efforts to government officials. In fact, one is more efficient if one keeps some distance from Mexican bureaucracy and learns to work within Mexican government guidelines.

Possibly, as a result of a strong sense of history and sensitivity to the presence of foreigners, Mexicans tend to look at the world outside their walls as hostile. U.S. citizens may be surprised to find that there is no real sense of commonwealth. Efforts to organize volunteers fail and charity, in the anonymous sense, is an alien idea. (Orphanages, for example, are the result of foreign aid.) Society functions through relationships of power and an individual's rights are determined by his/her level of influence. As a result, bossiness is responded to with conciliation and confrontation is thereby avoided.

There is no average Mexican and each region, each ethnic group, needs to be separately addressed. However, it has been said that one can expect to find a person who is both meditative and philosophical; one who is also discreet, evasive, and a bit distrustful. Mexicans tend to be proud and, like the Spanish portion of their roots, their literature suggests a nation that is consumed by questions of honor.

The most important issue to note, though, is that many Mexicans are traditional, internally set in their ways and, while externally anarchistic, are guided by tradition, not principles when it comes to relationships. The economic collapse in the early 1980s only cemented these feelings that the U.S. way of life is not predestined for Mexico.

People from the U.S. sometimes have trouble understanding Mexican "stubbornness" of this sort. As historian Josephine Zoraida Vázquez wrote, when discussing the separation of Texas from Mexico and the 1847 invasion,

> . . . in spite of their need for money, (the Mexicans) refused to sell uninhabited land, which they would lose anyway. But in addition to the conviction on the part of (Mexican) Presidents concerning the impossibility of selling "national patrimony," there existed a strong feeling of national pride which felt a near obligation to respond with arms to multiple American insults. (in "los primeros tropiezos," *Historia General de México*, El Colegio de México, 1976, p. 818)

Mexican culture, unlike U.S. national culture, is not one to produce team atheletes. The country has produced many more world famous boxers than soccer players, and there are more Mexican tennis heroes than basketball stars. One can witness a tremendous inner strength coming from a need for solitude, so popular in Mexican literature, and resulting in a creativity which has, historically, been expressed in art (pottery, weaving, metalwork, woodwork, color, food, and song).

The issue of solitude is extremely important in Mexico. Octavo Paz discusses Mexican reticence as a means of covering up thoughts and refers to the use of falsehood and euphemism in the language, as well as other misleading behavior, as endeavoring to hide true character. He refers to this behavior as "the mask."

This reticence, Paz and others suggest, may also come from a national inferiority complex, developed from years of conquest and racial commingling. Nevertheless, U.S. citizens would do well to realize that Paz's theories are highly controversial and have never been documented.

UNWRITTEN COMMUNICATIONS

Our messages are both written and unwritten, spoken and unspoken. The way we refer to and about others suggests more about ourselves and our own beliefs than our neighbors. When dealing with a mask, such as the fictitious Mexican identity that Octavio Paz has suggested–which is a basic part of the Mexican character–it becomes particularly important to understand the implicit meanings behind explicit speech.

Titles

Nobility was banished with the 1910 Revolution. *Don* and *doctor* and other common titles, or *licenciado*, will have a sphere of influence; individuals tend to dress the part, wearing a suit and tie as evidence of being "white-collar." Academic achievement, while important, is less so than social style. Deference is given and the article, *El*, is used to suggest supremacy. *Maestro*, or teacher, is used by and for the extremely skilled. Senior officials, while not full-time university professors, may teach in order to use this title.

Formal Language and Slang

The Mexican language has a life of its own. Prehistoric paintings show speech balloons (used in cartoons) detached in front of speakers. The ability to speak well is of great importance and, as with any flowery speech, empty promises come easily: they have no intrinsic value of their own.

At the other extreme, excessive frankness and directness is considered rude. Substantive discussions must be proceeded by small talk about family, politics, and so forth. One must learn to relate without confrontation and so in public life, senior officials expect flattery and aspiring politicos can launch into oratory at a moment's notice.

Official discourse is not direct but used to defend principle and values. Grandiose phrases are common in platform speeches and even in messages painted on walls. The real political message is conveyed in a code, so to speak, making reference to inside issues, generally obscure to anyone not in-the-know. Newspapers publish interviews rather than analysis as a copout; the lack of analysis makes the discussions hard to understand for their "real" meaning. It is also important for people from the U.S. to note that public lectures, whether historical, political, or sociological, will not admit to any failure of the system, and so most academic treatises about Mexico tend to be written by foreigners.

Formality, though, is first expressed in one's greeting. One offers one's name followed by the phrase, *para servirle* (ready to serve you). Additionally, self reference may be made in the third person (*su servidor*, or your service). Formally, speakers may describe their home as *su casa* (your house), the proper response being a mumbled *Gracias*.

Meanings are tucked into phrases, lines, pauses, emphasis and intonation, odd sounds, and gestures. Jokes made may be self-mocking or derogatory about Mexico in general, but it is imperative to understand that denigration is to be seen as nothing other than sarcastic. Just as friends may verbally joust with each other, one would never, as an outsider, venture participation.

PEOPLE FROM THE UNITED STATES SPEAKING SPANISH

U.S. citizens should realize that it is not advisable to translate an English business statement directly into the Spanish especially by using a dictionary. The traditions of writing business communications in Spanish are both old and complex and the terminology for business letters constitutes a complete subject of study in and of itself. To give a complete list of such technical terminology is beyond the scope of this book since entire volumes have been written on the correct forms for business Spanish.

Nevertheless, basic forms of address should be noted, such as Dear Sir (*Muy Señor Mío*) and Dear Madam (*Muy Señora Mía*), while the term for "dear" in business letters is always *Estimado* rather then the related term for "dear" (*querido*) which is used in personal letters.

The ending of business letters in Spanish is quite variable; however, it is worthy of note that the direct translation of the English word "sincerely" is almost never used, rather the word *atentamente* is generally used in its place.

The U.S. businessperson will find that his or her Mexican counterpart may very likely be bilingual, and this is almost certainly the case at the higher levels of business, professional, and government life. Nevertheless, there is no guarantee that this will always be the case, nor, on due reflection is there any reason why it should be.

Although English has become an international language, the United States no longer stands unchallenged in today's world of business. Foreigners, including Mexicans, will be very pleased that U.S. visitors make an attempt to speak their language. Unfortunately, it is very possible that the values of U.S. efficiency and pragmatism come into play here in a negative way.

All too often U.S. citizens think to themselves, "Why should I try to speak that language when I cannot really speak it fluently?" Americans sometimes feel that they must speak perfectly, or not at all. Although considerable accuracy is imperative for high-level international negotiations and preparing and using contracts and other legal documents, in the social communication of everyday life, perfection is neither needed nor expected. On the contrary, every word that is communicated is valuable in and of itself.

Above all, this knowledge of the language must be seen within a wider context. Mexicans take offense at U.S. cultural self-centeredness and they feel that U.S. education–as a product of U.S. culture–produces technically competent, but culturally shallow individuals. Since Mexicans give great importance to the creation of personal relationships as the basis for business, it will both impress and flatter the Mexican businessperson to see that his or her U.S. counterpart has taken the time and interest to learn his language and something about his world.

GESTURES

Body language can express more than the spoken or written word. Gestures such as chewing gum, failing to make eye contact with others during a conversation, slapping down a paper on a desk in front of someone else's view, speaking while one's feet are on a desk, stretching in public or speaking with ones' hands clasped behind the neck, are all gestures that may be resented by Mexicans. Worst of all they can make Mexicans feel that the U.S. visitor is either deliberately trying to insult them, or that the visitor is so ill-mannered that s/he is not sufficiently educated to be worth doing business with.

It is important to be able to read facial expressions and physical displays of interest and intent. Basically, the subtleties are similar in Mexican and U.S. cultures. However, some gestures are different from those found in the United States. Some of the most notable Mexican gestures are:

1. hand clenched and thumb stuck up vertically: a thumbs up sign means "good luck or well done";
2. fingertips held up to lips means "delicious";
3. fingertips closed to meet the tip of the thumb with all the fingers held together upwards while the hand in moved back and forth gives emphasis to the speaker's comments as if to say, "You'd better believe it";
4. fingertip placed under the center of one eye signifies "Be careful! Watch out!"
5. back of fingers brushed against the underside of the chin as fingers are thrust forward signifies "I couldn't care less."

WRITTEN COMMUNICATIONS

All forms of communications should begin with two questions: "What am I trying to accomplish?" and "How can I best accomplish it?" To that end, business writing should be seen as communication that attempts to influence the recipient.

Business letters are generally a substitute for direct contact. Their purpose is to save time and to get something done: to introduce a person or new business, to take an order or make a sale, to establish credit or collect money, to clear up a misunderstanding, or to build or retain goodwill. It is important to always keep in mind that the readers are *people*, rather than merely positions or names.

In Mexico, the writing style of business letters often includes many more pat or stock phrases–along with circumlocutions and subordinate clauses–than are usually found in U.S. business letters. With their traditional pragmatism, those from the U.S. like to get right to the point while Mexicans like to fill their business correspondence with lofty sounding phrases which may seem out of place to someone from the U.S. Indeed, Mexicans who read U.S. business letters for the first time may experience a kind of culture shock when realizing just how cut and dry businesspeople from the U.S. can be.

It is not recommended that U.S. businesspeople try to imitate the complex literary-business style that Mexicans use when writing business letters. The structure of Spanish business letters is rather an arcane subject and the visiting businessperson in Mexico would be better off using local talent to do the writing. As mentioned, entire books are written on this subject and he or she would do well to take a formal course in the subject if possible. Short of this, improvising a paraphrase of what a correct letter would really be like might be a mistake that could lead to embarrassment, misunderstanding, or even disaster.

The form of a letter should receive attention and, at times, can become sticky. The date should be placed directly below the letterhead, at the upper right or left hand side of the page, at least two spaces above the first line of the inside address. Unlike the U.S. method where the month precedes the day, Mexicans follow the European format and place the day first, then the month and year. After one becomes accustomed to this approach, it should be appreciated, as it omits the need for additional commas.

The inside address should be written exactly as it is on the company's stationery or advertising. This should provide some guideline for the salutation.

Salutations in Mexican business letters are not unlike those used in the U.S. It should always agree with the first line of the inside address: if the first line is plural or feminine, the salutation should be as well. Sometimes it is desirable to direct the letter to a specific individual not named in the inside address. In cases such as this, an attention getting device should be applied, such as *Atención:* followed by the person's full name and title.

Letters of Introduction

Because letters of introduction are formal, they do not have to be cold, and three things have to be accomplished.

1. The letter must offer the full name of the person being introduced.
2. It must offer a satisfactory reason for the intrusion.
3. It must make the recipient interested in and desirous of meeting the individual.

Letters of introduction must also allow an "out" in case the introduction is not desired and it must close with sincere thanks.

Sales Letters

Sales letters tend to follow a simple formula: gain attention, arouse interest, build desire, and call for action. However, this is a lot more difficult to do than it may appear on the surface. It is important to remember that attention is gained differently in different cultures, and gaining attention at the risk of offending the reader does more damage than good. Mexican culture emphasizes hospitality and sympathy. One should try to begin by talking, rather than writing, and vocabulary should be carefully checked to ensure that words have a pleasant meaning to the reader.

Good manners are more important than dignity. Expressing concern for the recipient's personal and business needs is very important. Referring to them by name or writing something about their city or specific business is very important in building trust and enhancing interest.

Desire is built by pleasing the reader. It is important to know the benefits the reader is seeking from the product, and the features and advantages pertinent to these benefits should be emphasized. A discussion of the way the product fits into the prospect's overall situation demonstrates sensitivity to the prospect's needs, and this is imperative in doing business in Mexico. U.S. businesspeople are seen as pushy and self-serving and an expression of interest in the Mexican prospect's well-being goes a long way.

Action is often not accomplished in a sales letter. The letter is merely considered to be an initial offer, requesting a response. It is important to leave some points unexplained or questions unanswered so that further contact will prove fruitful. One must create a desire to know more or to see the product in action so that an ensuing sales call is an enticement.

Credit and Collection Letters

Collection letters have two jobs: to collect money and retain goodwill. Many get so wrapped up in the first order of business that they overlook the importance of the second. The issue of the prospect's honor must be considered above all else and, on all occasions, a late or nonpayment is always referred to as an "oversight." The posture of such a letter is that payment is intended and an expression of thanks in advance is extremely important. Hints at unhappy consequences or of late or nonpayment are to be avoided.

There is a procedure to follow as well as assumptions to be made when informing customers about delinquent payments. One should assume, first, that the customer really wants to be reminded that payment is due and that s/he has forgotten to pay. Another assumption is that the seller has overlooked or needs to be informed of something and that the late payment is an indirect message to that extent. Courtesy and patience require that these assumptions be tested before stronger measures are taken.

Clearing up Misunderstandings

Apology letters can be categorized as letters of regret, letters in which the request is granted, and letters in which the request is denied. Apologies must be made with sincerity and regret. Amends must be offered and made whenever possible. One must also promise that the situation will not recur and thank the recipient for his/her tolerance and understanding.

When dealing with a complaint, one must put oneself in the complainant's shoes and avoid belittling them. It is important to admit guilt when necessary and make amends as soon as possible. The writer should show appreciation for hearing about the problem instead of receiving some action. It suggests alertness and even-handedness.

Along the same lines, one must make every effort to demonstrate tolerance when addressing a misunderstanding. We all make mistakes and an error on the part of another is no excuse for discourtesy. When one needs to complain, s/he should begin with a very specific explanation of what is wrong: exact dates, amounts, model numbers, colors, or any other specific information that makes rechecking easier for the recipient. A statement of the inconvenience or loss that has resulted from the error should be included as an appeal to the reader's sense of honor and justice. A direct statement as to what adjustment is considered fair is also needed and should be viewed as the beginning of a negotiation and a "first offer."

Facts, rather than emotion, appeal to the Mexican businessperson. Arguments based on historical precedent demonstrate knowledge of the business and its existence apart from one's own. Historical precedent approaches the issue from a grander scale, a less personal one, and suggests that personal issue will not be taken in this business dealing. In short, it is more courteous.

Goodwill Letters

Goodwill letters come in an assortment of types, from letters of acknowledgment and confirmation to letters of congratulations and appreciation. Letters of sympathy may also fall into this category as might letters of announcement and invitation.

Acknowledgement, or thank-you letters are written to provide documentation of something received. They should be as prompt as possible and specify what has been received in terms of exact dates (and times), amount, model numbers, color and any other information needed to check the item or inventory. They should also convey a direct thanks to the person to whom the letter is being written, but should be kept short since longer letters have a tendency to appear less than sincere.

Confirmation letters should offer exact dates, prices, figures, etc., needed to document an agreement. Sometimes confirmation letters are merely verification of a telephone conversation. If confirmation is sought, one might offer alternate dates, times, etc., to aid the recipient.

Congratulatory letters often come under the heading of public relations. These must be enthusiastic and friendly as well as sincere, showing no envy for the recipient's condition. One must say nothing to detract from the accomplishment, whether it be a marriage, birth, promotion, new job, book, or personal achievement, such as the receipt of an award or civic office.

Sympathy letters need to be brief. Care must be taken that they are not macabre and one should avoid tales of one's own troubles. Assistance should be offered, when realistic, and the form should not be overly flowery or sentimental.

Announcements should be made at once and one must take care to be specific about time, dates, titles, company names, and addresses. After the initial information is provided one may elaborate with background material to add importance to the announcement.

Invitations should tell why an event is taking place (for example, to honor someone, introduce someone, or set off a campaign), as well as when and where the event will take place. Information about whether dinner or lunch will be provided needs to appear as well as the hour of arrival. One should ask for acceptance or refusal by a given date in the form of an RSVP.

Memoranda

Memoranda are used to accomplish a number of things. First, they maintain a flow of information across levels of an organization. Second they convey information both up and down the levels of an organization. Third, they serve as reminders and, as a result, provide permanent documentation of discussions, meetings, activities, changes, procedures, and policies. It becomes, then, worthwhile to prepare them with care.

Memos should be short and to the point. Additionally, interoffice communications should be as polite as communications with a customer. They should be clear and graphic, offering an explanation of what is going to be done and how it will be accomplished, and providing a summary and/or drawing conclusions or making recommendations regarding the action/s described. Memos should also offer an opportunity for further discussion if necessary. A thank-you should be offered for anticipated cooperation, as well as a word of praise, if possible.

A FINAL WORD

A fitting conclusion to this chapter includes a short list of some Mexican slang terms. A complete list of Mexican words and expression can and does fill weighty tomes, however the observations listed below may give the U.S. visitor a flavor of the color and subtlety with which language is used in Mexico.

Names are very important in Mexico. Drinking places are often given witty names, such as The Four Winds, Stop Brother, or Fearless John. Drugstores may be named after saints and bakeries or groceries may be given inspirational names (for example, *La Esperanza*, Hope). Even pushcarts for ice cream or candies can have cute names. Cheap eating places can be named–in tongue-in-cheek fashion–after famous restaurants. Trucks and buses sometimes receive sentimental and humorous names as do paintings of small images.

Nicknames are extremely popular and they often have a contrary or ironical twist. Lighter eyed or haired people are sometimes called *El Güero* (for a male) or *La Güera* (for a female), meaning the blond one (no you will not find these words in a standard Spanish dictionary). Such nicknames are often used instead of a person's Christian name by family or friends.

Slang is sometimes quite clever:

No te hagas guaje (Literally, "don't make a gourd of yourself," or, in other words, "don't play innocent [with me].")

Codo (elbow; means stingy. The gesture accompanying this phrase includes doubling the left arm and touching the elbow with the right hand.)

Yó tengo mis dientes (I already have my eyeteeth. Point to one's eyeteeth with one's fingers to mean "I wasn't born yesterday.")

Yo Colón ("I'm Columbus," accompanied by pointing the forefinger to the right eye. It's like the U.S. expression "I'm from Missouri, show me," meaning, I'm skeptical.)

Hacer la barba (To fix one's face means to flatter. The hand gesture is done by rubbing the right cheek with the back of the right hand.)

Ni modo (Who cares?)

Andale (This is, perhaps, the most disconcerting expression for non-Mexicans since it can mean so many things, but it generally means "Hurry up!")

One must be careful of insults. Fool, idiot, and rascal are commonplace insults. *Sinvergüenza* means shameless one, or simply a person who is no good, and *hijo* can be loosely translated as "jerk." There are also a number of Indian curses one should become familiar with if traveling or working in areas where Indian cultures are prevalent.

Finally, many Mexican sayings are sometimes very similar to those used in the U.S. Mexicans say, "A bird in the hand is worth more than a hundred in the air," "Much noise but few nuts" (for "All that glitters is not gold"), and "A saint who is not seen is not worshipped" ("Out of sight, out of mind"). A ceaseless talker is referred to as talking "even through his/her elbows." Finally, "Only he who does not mount does not fall," or "Nothing ventured, nothing gained."

The U.S. visitor who experiences the richness and endless variations of words and expressions in the Mexican language cannot help but be impressed by the incredible complexity of the Spanish language itself which manifests itself in many guises throughout the Spanish-speaking world. The linguistic varieties within Spanish literally take millions of forms. The language is truly endless and no human being, whether Mexican or otherwise, can completely master local subtleties of the Spanish language in every Hispanic country. This fact, alone, should impress the U.S. visitor with the knowledge that the Mexican language is as rich and complex as English. One should also realize that Mexico is very proud of sharing the Hispanic literary tradition. A truly mutual respect along all these lines will go a long way toward solidifying personal relations through many areas of international business.

Chapter 6

Management in Mexico

A CASE HISTORY

A foreign visitor to Mexico came to a business office wearing Mexican huarache sandals that he had bought at a local Indian market. When in Rome do as the Romans do, he thought.

No one at the office said a word to him, but the cold stares he got told him that he had committed an unpardonable faux pas. He learned the hard way that there is a great difference between acceptable dress in the country at a native market and in an office, particularly one that deals in international business.

DRESS

Perhaps the greatest challenge for the foreigner working in Mexico is the mastery of the problems presented by intercultural management. These come under many headings; however, one of the areas most likely to cause problems is dress. Acceptable dress in Mexico, will, of course, vary from situation to situation and location to location. Urban areas, particularly, Mexico City, tend, naturally, to be more formal than the villages and highlands. City dress is also more formal than dress in tropical and coastal areas. Indian culture is expressed in dress, but by natives, only. U.S. businesspeople attempting to adorn themselves in Indian costume will look, at best, like tourists. However, it might be a worthwhile foray to explore some of the dress customs found in native Mexico.

Indian Dress

Dress differs by region and in Mexico dress sometimes appears to be a high expression of art. Prior to the Spanish conquest, Indians wore colorful garments, painted their faces, and wore jewelry made of gold and precious stones. Centuries of poverty and suffering have not totally suppressed this part of the culture and some bright color has been preserved in much indigenous dress.

Women may dress more traditionally, with full, flounced skirts reaching to their ankles or sweeping the ground. The waist may be plain or yoked. Some sleeveless *camisas* or white cotton shirts embroidered with silk thread or beads may be worn tucked inside the skirt.

Children's dresses are like their mothers'. Modern dresses are often made of inexpensive, colorful prints sold in city markets. Some village women wear costumes reminiscent of preconquest days.

There are two types of preconquest blouses: the *quexquemetl*, two rectangular pieces of cloth joined to form points, hung over the shoulders like a cape; and *huipils*, square-necked, sleeveless, loose and shapeless blouses, which may vary in length. Skirts, *enaguas*, include the *enredo*, a wraparound made of homespun wool, pleated at the waist in the front or back, and fastened with *fajas*, homespun sashes or belts. Otomi women around Toluca might wear *chinquetes*, hand woven woolen skirts, pleated in front and held by a red wool sash with a woven design and a *quexquemetl*. Styles, of course, differ by region.

Young Indian girls often wear their hair loose or in braids hanging down the back. Married women wind the braids around their heads or coil them in the back.

Native footwear is a male item. Regardless of the elegance of the clothing, women in Indian dress tend to be barefoot (although shoes may be worn for dancing). Women do not wear hats, except, perhaps while working in the field. At that point a woman may don a man's sombrero.

Indian men can be seen wearing unbleached cotton suits, shirts and trousers of the same color. Sometimes the shirt is rose-colored, orange, purple, or yellow. Regional differences can be found in the cut of the pants (pleated at the sides, fuller, etc.) and shirts (plain, yoked, pleated, cross-stitched, or embroidered). Long sashes of homespun wool or red cotton are sometimes tied around the waist.

In the city, however, traditional suits are worn. Still, straw sombreros may be seen.

The sarape or blanket, worn as an overcoat, varies from region to region. The *jorongo* is medium-sized, and is folded over the left shoulder as an adornment. *Tilmas* or *cotones* are like *chamarras* (short jackets) of Chiapas. Full-sized sarapes are used for protection.

Men's hair is generally worn short, but some wear it long like the Lacandons, Seris, Huichols, or Tarahomaras; however, men's hair is never braided. The Huichols, Tarahomaras, and some others may wear headbands.

Girls and women may adorn their outfits and/or hair with inexpensive beads of all colors. Up to a dozen strands at a time are not unusual. Some beads tend to be expensive, such as the gold ones worn in Yucatan, and the silver ones.

The Huichols and Seris may paint their faces with designs and colors. Huichol men often wear earrings, bracelets, hairbands, and plumes or even flowers at fiestas. The Maya at Quintana Roo wear one gold earring in the left ear.

Cleanliness is subcultural. Generally, the Mexican Indians are frequent bathers and heavily perfumed (especially the men). It is important that one not offend others with one's personal presentation. On the other extreme, the Huichols may take only occasional ritual baths and clothing may be worn until it literally falls off the body.

GROOMING FOR BUSINESS

Grooming, hair, makeup and fragrances are important symbols of one's station in life. As a result, a good deal of care should be taken with one's appearance. Hair should be meticulously kept and makeup freshened. Those handling money should dress conservatively. Those involved in creative endeavors, for example intellectuals, may dress more for comfort than style. While some regions and settings are more formal than others, it is important to note that, overall, Mexicans follow European fashion more closely than U.S. fashion.

The best way to learn how to dress in another culture is to

observe others closely. As correct dress can forward a career, inappropriate dress can arrest it and, while it may seem unfair that something so superficial should be so important, it, nevertheless, is. To simplify matters, one needs to watch his or her Mexican work environment closely to ensure that:

1. one's dress is typical of others at the same level in the company;
2. one's clothing tends toward the traditional, rather than the stylistic;
3. one's clothing is appropriate to his or her body build (many U.S. businesspeople both feel and look uncomfortable in European-cut clothing/suits), and;
4. the fabric chosen is of top quality, a nuance noted in Mexican middle- and upper-class circles.

Mexican women tend to wear more makeup than women in the U.S. Nails are worn a bit longer than in the U.S. and they are almost always "done," or polished, rather than worn bare. Both men and women use fragrances, much more so than the typical U.S. resident. Mornings in the office can be an experience in a mixture of fragrance. In short, Mexicans pay very close attention to not merely being clean, but smelling so. They are much more conscious of aroma and the possibility of offending another.

For help, U.S. businesspeople might benefit from spending some time with a fashion consultant in urban specialty clothing stores. The less expensive route, however, is doing what one might do at home: locating a peer who has obvious fashion sense.

Finally, one should always leave the office looking just as "put together" as when s/he arrived. After all, for many, going to and coming from work are the most public times of the day.

Male Wardrobe

City men wear suits, not sports coats, to work, usually with a white shirt and tie. Suits are cut in a more fitted European fashion than the boxy U.S. cuts. While white is the preferential color for men's dress shirts, light blue, off-white, or pale green are acceptable; pinks and violets are considered feminine colors.

Shoes are of fine leather and, as in the corporate United States, Italian loafers are quite acceptable. It is important to note that Mexicans are more like Parisians in their recognition of style than those from the U.S. They are more likely to notice the quality of clothing worn and accessories used than the average U.S. citizen and as one colleague pointed out to the authors, "In Mexico, you get treated as well as you dress; the better you dress, the better you're treated."

It is also important to wear dark socks. As in the U.S., a flash of leg when one sits is considered slovenly.

Upper-class Mexican men wear relatively little jewelry, generally only a fine watch and a ring. Heavy bracelets and necklaces are considered lower class, or *naco*, and one is, potentially, looked down upon.

Men keep their jackets on in Mexico. Even when it is very hot, jackets are worn in public, around one's superiors, and in front of one's clients or anyone from outside the office. If one tends to remove a jacket during the course of the work day, s/he should remember to wear long-sleeved shirts. Double-breasted jackets are always to be worn buttoned.

While it is not the intent of the authors to appear crude, it must be noted that a view of a man's undershirt, when he is relaxing with his collar open, is as inappropriate as the sight of a woman's slip or bra strap. Currently, it is not in vogue for there to be any indication of an undershirt. People from the U.S. are used to seeing the heavy white on white look, but Mexicans, like Europeans, tend to soften the look by not wearing T-shirts.

Female Wardrobe

As more Mexican women assume greater positions of responsibility and power, female executive dress becomes increasingly prescribed. Women wear business suits, in general, and dress tends to cover up both the arms and upper legs. Pantsuits are now acceptable in the office, but clothing must be coordinated.

Accessories worn during the work day are simple and heels tend to be higher than those worn in U.S. offices. However, it is common for women to wear sneakers or walking shoes to and from the office. Women carry purses and, in Mexico City, umbrellas. It is expected that a woman's shoes, purse, and umbrella be color coordinated.

Mexican women tend to wear a bit more jewelry than their counterparts in the U.S. Not only is hair meticulously combed, but dress and accessories are carefully coordinated. Earrings are generally always worn, and women tend to accessorize with a necklace or pin, a bracelet, and watch, even for work. However, as in the U.S., jewelry should be noiseless in the office.

Casual Wear

Casual dress in Mexico is not the same as "casual" dress in the U.S., often mistaken for "come as you are." At a weekend daytime outing, men wear slacks and sports shirts and women, skirts or slacks and blouses. However, it is important to note that some men are still uncomfortable around women in pants. Jeans, while worn by the young, are not considered proper business casual wear. If in doubt about proper dress for an event, it is not considered impolite, especially for a visitor to Mexico, to ask the host or hostess. A late afternoon/early evening party may involve a set or two of tennis or drinks around the pool.

Casual clothing, like office wear, should be of top quality fabric and current fashion. Shoes should be carefully polished and clothing should be neat and pressed. When leisure time is spent in the company of business colleagues, the company image is involved, and so all the rules of formal public appearance are to be followed.

Under no condition (except, of course, as a tourist) should men or women appear in public in shorts. For Mexican adults, shorts are considered attire suitable only as beach wear.

Finally, if one is mid- to senior-level management, it is best to be prepared to wear evening clothes. Even if a black-tie or formal event has not been placed on one's itinerary, it may well (and commonly will) arise. Finding a suitable clothier that can make alterations in short order is difficult in any strange city, let alone in one's own country. Doing so in another country, and cultural setting, can prove to be a true chore.

In short, Mexicans tend to dress more formally on all occasions. Women are dressed, in heels and stockings, even for trips to the grocers. They accompany their young children to the school bus fully madeup and dressed as though for work. Basically, whether in the garden, on the street, or doing Saturday chores, Mexicans tend to take great care in their public appearance.

Some Dos and Don'ts

Here are a few dos and don'ts for dressing in Mexico.

1. Never wear shorts in public, except at the beach. Shorts are reserved for tourists and children and are not modest enough for adults.
2. Women should note that sundresses–those with straps or low/ cut tops–should be put in the same category as shorts: off limits in the city.
3. Men should be careful not to wear too much jewelry. People from the southwestern U.S. tend to wear much more than would be expected and will stand out the same way someone in Western garb stands out in the Northeast.
4. Fragrances, for both men and women, are important and should be worn.
5. Running shoes are fine for walking to and from work, but are out of place in the office.
6. Men should take care to wear conservative colored shirts and ties: pinks and violets are out.
7. Visitors from the U.S. should dress in their own clothing. Attempting to fit into a European cut of clothing makes one not only feel, but act, awkward.
8. Men with hair in modern styles, such as a ponytail, shaved sides, etc., will almost certainly become the subject of ridicule. If there is one sure way to make a bad impression in Mexico, it is by presenting this type of appearance.
9. U.S. tourists who become overly fascinated with a tourist's version of Mexican clothing (gigantic, round Mexican hats often embroidered in gold or silver, or brightly colored sarapes) will only succeed in appearing to be tourists (and not very sophisticated tourists at that). It is important not to go overboard when it comes to adopting what appears to be the local style of dress. When in doubt one should watch what his/her local Mexican business colleagues are wearing.

10. Along the same lines visitors may sometimes find that Mexicans in more rural areas wear what U.S. visitors would consider to be cowboy boots. However, adopting such clothing in urban areas, such as Mexico City, is inappropriate. Mexico City (as has been frequently mentioned in this book) is a sophisticated, modern city, not unlike its counterparts in Europe and the United States. Cowboy boots and other typically rural clothing, just like in the U.S., marks one as a "country bumpkin" who is trying to make it in the big city.

11. Men would do well to stick to dark colors for their suits. While tans and even whites are acceptable (in tropical areas) darker suits make a better impression and are more common in offices.

NEGOTIATION

Negotiations take place daily and whether at the market, home, workplace, or boardroom, similar rules apply. First, one's asking price is, simply, the price asked, and it is expected to be, initially, too high. A response to this effect, albeit euphemistic or, to varying degrees, indirect, is generally expected. It then becomes the responsibility of the respondent to make an offer, showing a genuine desire to buy.

It is important, in Mexico, that negotiations remain friendly and conciliatory. Negotiators should smile and act friendly toward one another. Tourists who bargain "to the bone," are not welcomed and border tourist markets often demonstrate a "take it or leave it" attitude stemming from a history of abusive actions.

Negotiating is an art, but skill in this form of communication can be improved with a few simple measures. First, intercultural negotiations require even more organization than intracultural negotiations. One must constantly be aware of how many different parties are involved in the issue to be resolved. The relationship of government and officialdom from business in the U.S. is not at all similar to the relationship in Mexico. While government has privatized any number of Mexican industries, numerous private interests still exist.

A second issue to consider when analyzing the parties involved in the negotiation is whether each party is centralized or independent. For example, in a U.S. company, a negotiating team may have to answer to a number of functions within an organization. This would hold true in Mexican business, as well. Workers and management alike are represented by separate unions.

It is also important to consider the uniqueness of the negotiated situation. If a sales agreement, for example, is to be arranged, the relationship will ideally become an ongoing one in which both sides are seeking a mutually agreeable position that can be defended during future sales meetings. If the situation is a one-time "deal," positions on each side tend to be exaggerated and more room for conciliation tends to exist than meets the eye. Additionally, if a negotiated decision impinges on upcoming negotiations, sides will tend to be more polarized and skilled negotiators will need to be able to tie these negotiations together, using each other for leverage. Sometimes negotiations are used for airing opinions or grievances and do not warrant agreement, just acknowledgment.

Time is a major issue in intercultural negotiations. Information-specific societies, like the U.S., tend to place far more importance on time spent than information-nonspecific cultures like Mexico do. The party that negotiates in haste is always at a clear disadvantage. Penalties occurring as a result of delays may be quite different for the negotiating parties.

The degree to which negotiations are private also plays an important role. Mexican culture does not permit criticism of traditional policies and positions in public, and speakers will not back down from a traditional stand. While public pronouncements, via leakages, can and have been employed, this is a dangerous game even in the most hospitable of relationships.

LABOR-MANAGEMENT RELATIONS

The foreign manager in Mexico must realize, first and foremost, that workers probably come from a culture very different from one's own. Even in urban areas, many workers have recently arrived from the countryside where modern devices such as telephones are relatively rare. Managers will have to make allowances for a period of acculturation and proper training in the use of basic appliances, as well as sophisticated machinery.

This culture shock is often mutual, however, and foreign managers need to become used to many legal and cultural differences. There is a common belief, for instance, that Mexico is far behind the United States and Western Europe in the area of worker's rights and, therefore, foreign businesses entering Mexico can pretty much make up their own labor rules and regulations. Nothing could be further from the truth, however, as Mexican labor law is comprehensive and far-reaching. Mexican workers, for example, have much greater job security than their U.S. counterparts and it is usually very difficult to fire Mexican workers after an initial trial period has elapsed. Mexican labor law is also strict in regard to Christmas bonuses (called *Aguinaldos*), and sick and pregnancy leaves. It is, therefore, imperative that foreign companies entering Mexico check with the appropriate Mexican legal counsel about such matters before beginning to do business.

Other areas of potential difficulty are much more subtle, since many practices and attitudes that are common in the United States will be unacceptable in Mexico. Many observers have noted that the Mexican worker is often more loyal to individuals than to organizations. This reality lays out a very clear challenge to the foreign manager in Mexico who cannot necessarily take workers' loyalty to the parent company for granted. In no way should this challenge suggest that the manager should try to over-extend him/herself in attempting to develop a warm or even informal relationship with company employees. On the contrary, research in cross-cultural management practices indicates that power distance is generally greater in Mexico than it is in the United States.

Rather than looking for the breezy informality that is often the hallmark of U.S. worker-managerial relations (informal joking with employees, cordial backslapping, and asking workers to address managers by their first names) may tend to cause confusion and even resentment on the part of Mexican workers. Mexican society is much more of a class-differentiated society and efforts to minimize class differences are not always welcome. As mentioned before, Mexicans are quick to point out that the superficial equality between U.S. managers and workers is often nothing but a sham and when the chips are down managers really feel no bond of friendship or loyalty toward their workers. Whether this is true or not, Mexican workers in one industry actually quit when they were asked to give feedback about their jobs. They felt that if their supervisors needed to ask, they were no longer in control and must, then, not really know their jobs.

In addition, workers south of the border have been found to feel uncomfortable with the more rigid requirements of U.S.- and European-style production. Mexicans are less used to being inspected at every stage of the production process. Quality control is generally a less-developed and much more informal art than it is in countries like the United States and Japan, and a system of worker appraisal is often a vague and badly defined one. In terms of the production of electrical products, for example, the UL rating itself, or production that meets UL standards, is less common in Mexico than it is in the United States. Additionally, understanding why a person would want to manufacture products that would meet this level of quality is also less common.

The same sense of urgency in production and deadlines seen in the U.S. and Japan is not as common in Mexico. Time commitments are generally much more flexible in Mexico.

Also, Mexicans tend to be reluctant to convey bad news, and that includes news about production delays and other business problems. These attitudes, undoubtedly products of a Hispanic sense of fatalism which has already been discussed, run throughout the culture and are not specific to workers alone but are qualities of managers and executives, as well.

Traditionally, speed and efficiency of mass production has not been as much of a concern for Mexican manufacturing as it has been in the United States. Again, this is a product of the culture that values a slower-paced, more humanistic approach to life, including business. Mexicans see those in the U.S. as being obsessed with machines and gadgets, even having an innate bias in favor of anything that is technological, if only in its nomenclature. As a result, Mexican manufacturing has been done on a smaller, less standardized scale, and managers have been less concerned about sending their workers off for training in the use of the latest device or for study of technological development. Rather than training being the key to survival and economic success, ingenuity is. Mexicans are famous for finding new ways to adapt machinery and equipment already at their disposal. Likewise, Mexican managers and workers have been known to be more resistant to highly organized forms of inventory management.

There are times when the human angle should take precedence over business-oriented, or mechanized efficiency. The foreign manager must remember how highly sensitive the Mexican is to criticism. Additionally, Mexican workers may be wary about foreigners coming into their plants telling them what to do and how to do it better. Above all else, a manager must never publically criticize one worker in front of another, nor should a manager make light of Mexican holidays or special occasions.

In effect, the foreign manager should remember that s/he is a guest in Mexico, and the local culture is a crucial matter to one's workers. Local culture should never be taken lightly. This idea may seem self evident, however, it is more vital than it may seem at first glance.

A foreign manager may be shocked and even frustrated in trying to get an urgent piece of business done during the Christmas or Easter season only to find out that these important holidays are not celebrated as only one day, rather they tend to encompass a whole season. S/he will find that little, if any business is conducted between the 18th or 20th of December until the New Year, and the sense of urgency that American culture gives to business during this time may indeed cause confusion and frustration.

This same manager may also find that Mexicans are more willing to interrupt business matters with personal concerns. This may also cause consternation on the foreigner's part, but it may also tempt him or her to adopt a condescending attitude toward Mexican business in general. This would be a great mistake, since these differences are simply reflections of culture.

It is also important to remember that Mexican society is more varied and less homogenized than U.S. society, so that holidays are not only national but regional and local. Visitors working outside of Mexico City will have to become familiar with local customs, as well as national ones, and this includes the observance of both holidays and holy days. The same is true of the daily schedule for meals and the work day in general. At least one U.S. company failed in Mexico because it tried to get Mexican workers to work on a U.S. schedule with a 12 to 1 lunch hour, which, (as the following chapter describes) is radically different from the Mexican custom.

OPTIMIZING A MEXICAN WORKFORCE

It is difficult to imagine how many companies have experienced management problems in Mexico. Employee turnover has been very high, particularly in border manufacturing plants or Maquiladoras. Nevertheless, clever and sensitive management personnel have been able to substantially reduce the effects of these problems and even turn them around by simply working with, rather than against, the culture and preferences of Mexican workers. Here are some suggestions and considerations for optimizing a Mexican labor force.

1. Family is of primary importance to Mexicans. Many workers have left their homes and families in rural areas to come to urban areas to find work. Successful foreign managers recognize that many of these workers eventually abandon their jobs to go back to their families. They have instituted enlightened leave policies so that workers can visit their families more often without having to make the difficult decision between work and family.

2. Requests for time off from work to attend to family matters often take on a different nature than those in the United States where such requests usually refer to a worker's immediate family. Foreign managers are often surprised to receive requests for time off because a niece, nephew, or cousin is sick. Such requests are legitimate and should be taken seriously by management. Refusal of this type of request can have a very negative effect on employee morale.

3. Because of the importance of family, including extended family, some successful managers have arranged transportation by bus, rail, etc., for groups of workers to visit their families in rural areas. Little else can have a more positive impact on worker morale than sensitivity to this issue.

4. Many of the manufacturing jobs that U.S. companies offer to Mexican workers are tedious. It is for this reason that the majority of the work force of Maquiladoras tend to be female. U.S. managers

have found that women tend to be more patient with labor intensive and repetitive manufacturing operations.

Another important consideration when supervising workers in this type of detailed work is that some workers need glasses in order to see the often minute components. Unfortunately, Mexican workers very often simply cannot afford glasses in light of the wages in Mexico, a country in which a pair of glasses can cost considerably more than in the United States. Providing glasses free of charge has been a real morale booster in certain border plants.

5. Because of the repetitive and, frankly, boring nature of many of these factory jobs, simply providing background music for employees has also made a big difference in employee morale and in reducing turnover problems.

6. By the same token, training workers for a variety of tasks and allowing them to vary their manufacturing tasks has gone a long way toward relief of worker boredom.

7. Creating a newsletter in Spanish about the company, featuring news about specific employees and specific operational sections of the company, has also proven to be an excellent way to make workers feel appreciated. Workers, themselves, may also publish their own newsletter, and this practice has greatly enhanced morale. The key is to publish a newsletter in the Spanish language, even if English is the language spoken on the job, and letting the employees have input into the editorial decisions.

Foreign managers will find, in general, that Mexican workers become extremely loyal and hard working, especially when they feel that their contributions to the success of their company are really appreciated by management. However, in order for a manager to gain this loyalty and trust s/he must show loyalty and trust in their workers.

Accordingly, Mexicans are effusive and expressive. It would be wise to be the same and make expressions of approval and thanks in clearly visible ways. A handshake should be strong and direct. When speaking with employees good eye contact and a positive tone of voice will go a long way toward establishing harmonious relations between management and labor.

8. Mexican society is less individualistically oriented than U.S. society, and Mexican workers function well in groups. Because of

the cultural differences already outlined, it is important for managers to give clear directions to their workers, allowing for an acculturation period relating to differing standards of time, production, etc.

Also, time spent in worker relationships with peers should be expected and even encouraged. Work done in groups should be arranged. At the same time, managers should moderate their innate bias in favor of very strict observance of time regulations and of completion of tasks with machine-like precision.

Finally, managers coming to work in Mexico should allow for their own culture shock, as well as for that of their families. They should expect to be off balance for the first few months of their employment. Much that they see and experience will be so new that they will themselves feel disoriented. As a result, one may be tempted to reject cultural differences as annoyances and become defensive, insisting things be done their way. To give in to such temptations would be the worst error that a manager could make. A manager should be forewarned that such an attitude may be a recipe for professional and commercial disaster.

Chapter 7

Entertaining

A CASE HISTORY

A person from the U.S. on business in Mexico was invited to a party at the house of a Mexican industrialist whose business he wanted very badly. Thinking that U.S. informality extended into Mexico, his wife decided to wear jeans to the party. On arriving at the house, she found that the Mexican women were dressed to the nines with elegant dresses and fine jewelry. Her appearance called more attention to the couple than they had planned and, as a result, this woman and her husband received a decidedly cold reception. The man's business in Mexico never really prospered after that.

As noted earlier in this book, Mexicans pay careful attention to the details of social life. Above and beyond specific cultural differences relating to the amenities of human relations, it is important for U.S. visitors to realize that the pragmatism of U.S. life again comes into play in the differing structure of etiquette relating to meals and social invitations. These subtle variations can all too often lead to cultural clashes which are regrettable and avoidable if U.S. visitors are made aware of deep-seated sensibilities that permeate the fabric of social relations.

TABLE MANNERS

It may be wise, first, to review what has generally been considered to be good manners. One may have slipped away from observing many of these precepts over time simply because colleagues in the more informal United States may not take offense at departing from the rule books. Because of this, one may be tempted to feel that whatever is acceptable in the United States is acceptable throughout the civilized world. After all, people from the U.S. like to believe that the United States sets the standards in this as in just about all else.

Such an attitude is a fatal flaw in one's basic preparation for business life in Mexico. A superior attitude in the matter of social etiquette comes through on one level or another and cannot be hidden, no matter how much one may try. One's Mexican counterparts will feel it with their sixth sense (after all, Latins *are* more intuitive than their U.S. counterparts) and will resent it.

Yet many mistakes that U.S. businesspeople have made in Mexico are not the result of attitude at all. Conversely, by desperately wanting to fit in and make a good impression, they make subtle and not so subtle social errors, based on a lack of understanding of the social differences between the two countries.

Following is a list of recommendations that can help in making the best impression possible at social events. Some of these ideas may seem arbitrary and strange. Others may appear to be extensions of elementary courtesy. However, they all constitute areas of conduct in which U.S. visitors *have* already experienced problems in Mexico at one time or another.

1. One should never put his/her elbows on the table.

Mexicans judge their guests on their table manners. It is important not to forget that, in the Latin culture, good education is much more than the degrees that a person holds. A well-educated person comports him or herself with the dignity befitting his or her professional position. Since people from the U.S. have the reputation of being boorish and insensitive to social niceties, it is all the more important for U.S. visitors to take care in the impression they leave.

2. One must not tilt one's chair backwards while seated.

This not only puts one in an awkward position, but it is also dangerous. At any rate, it is considered crude in Mexico.

3. One must never stretch at the table.

In order to grasp the importance of this idea, one may wish to remember the story of a businessman from Indiana who lost an important deal in Mexico. His hosts were insulted that he stretched his arms and clasped his hands behind his head after he had finished his dinner but was still seated at the table.

4. Men should never take their jackets off at the dinner table when eating in public.

The only exceptions to this rule would occur when eating a meal at an informal fast-food restaurant or during a meal at a tropical locale. It is important to note and avoid the popular U.S. stereotype of Mexico, that suggests that all of Mexico is tropical, especially Mexico City. Mexico is a large country and its climate varies greatly from one region to another and Mexico City does *not* have a tropical climate. When studying the variety of weather patterns within Mexico, one should consider that the city of Cuernavaca, only an hour's drive from Mexico City, has four distinct weather zones despite that city's relatively small size.

Additionally, most restaurants in Mexico City and other large urban areas still ask that male patrons wear a jacket and tie, and all upscale urban restaurants are air conditioned in the summer months.

5. One, particularly men, should not compliment Mexican colleagues on their spouse's appearance during a social engagement.

The reason for this should be obvious. Nevertheless, a lack of sensitivity to Mexican psychology may leave many U.S. business-people confused about the principle of etiquette that is operating here. Suffice to say that the Mexican is possessive and has been known to be more jealous than many people from the U.S. think may be reasonable or justified. This orientation is not one of reason, but rather, one of culture and attitude, and the U.S. visitor is on foreign ground. Visitors would do well to remember the old Spanish saying, *"Por donde fueres, haz lo que vieres"* (When in Rome do as the Romans do).

6. Guests should neither rush through the meal nor rush to be the first to begin eating.

Latins generally enjoy lingering over a long meal. The U.S. invented the concept of the fast-food restaurant and this is only logical since people from the U.S. tend to think of food as simply a means to an end. Mexicans, however, tend to enjoy food in and of itself, as an end in itself, and for the social possibilities of extended conversation. It is perhaps worthy of note that the Spanish expression for after dinner conversation, *conversacíon de sobremesa* is an important part of the culture.

7. One must not be too quick to talk shop after beginning a meal.

Mexicans like to linger over the social aspects of their meal, as well, before they begin to talk business. Likewise, U.S. visitors should not be disconcerted when they find that Mexicans can radically shift the subject and tone of their conversations and begin to talk business, then shift to philosophy, religion, sports, politics, the arts, or whatever, all the while weaving business matters in and out of these subjects.

This cultural difference reflects a different view of life. Latins have a wider view of life, seeing it as a whole composed of many parts each of which are vitally important.

U.S. visitors may also find that Mexicans can go from the ridiculous to the sublime in the twinkling of an eye. This is incredible to many U.S. citizens who have been trained to see life in neat little compartments. Mexican temperament finds life to be too diverse to lend itself to scientifically, or most often, pseudo-scientifically oriented categories.

U.S. businesspeople should be prepared for these jumps in theme and tone and they should *never* interpret them as a lack of seriousness on the Mexicans' part nor should they think that they personally are not being taken seriously.

8. Mexicans often let their social events go until very late in the evening.

It is not uncommon for parties to go until the wee hours of the following morning. Some Mexicans will even party all night and go without sleep before their next day at work.

People from the U.S., on the other hand, rarely stay much after midnight while attending social events during the work week. In order to present the best social form, however, it would be best not to be the first guest to leave a social event.

All eyes tend to be on the foreign guest, and if s/he leaves too early, the departure may be interpreted as a lack of willingness to join in the fun or a sign of disapproval of the local customs, food, drink, entertainment, or music.

9. Mexicans generally prefer business luncheons to business breakfasts.

Mexicans like to linger for several hours over their lunch which is the main meal of the day. As a result, this event is an ideal time to discuss business matters.

If one is having lunch with a high-ranking official of a Mexican company, one should not feel that s/he is keeping him from his high-level, executive responsibilities if lunch takes two hours. Overconcern about time will show through in patterns of speech, constant glances at one's watch, or in facial expression. This may be interpreted as unwillingness to spend time with the official.

Additionally, one should not feel, however, that, in order to fit in with Mexican colleagues one must like hot, spicy Mexican food. Mexican cities are as cosmopolitan in their variety of cuisines as any U.S. city. As a matter of fact, one's Mexican counterparts will probably order from a truly international menu unless Mexican cuisine is specifically indicated as a preference. Also, Mexican cuisine itself is incredibly varied, changing from state to state and region to region. Finally, not all Mexican cuisine is the same as the Mexican food found in the United States. Acknowledging this fact will duly impress your Mexican hosts.

Mexican lunch is eaten between 1:30 and 3:30 p.m. and it is generally a very heavy meal. Except for formal dinner engagements, when a complete meal is served, supper is generally eaten between 7:00 and 10:30 p.m. and is very light.

Wine is a very popular drink with meals offered in someone's home, and a bottle of wine is, of course, always very suitable as a dinner gift. Imported wine, particularly European, is especially appreciated.*

Mexico does produce wine and it can be very good. Nevertheless Mexicans have a sharp eye for and greatly appreciate wine, sherry, cognac, and other liquors from Europe. They tend to appreciate them even more than people from the U.S. do since imported goods were not available for many years in Mexico, or were only available at astronomical prices.

10. Mexicans are not generally as much in the habit of sending thank-you cards after a social invitation as Americans are.

Mail service in Mexico is not as dependable as the U.S. mail service and it is generally a lot slower. One should not send invitations to social events by mail and expect them to get there on time. There is a good chance they will not. Instead, invitations should be made in person or by phone.

Mexicans are very vocal in expressing their thanks to a host, both at the end of a social event and in their subsequent conversations after the social engagement is over. For obvious reasons, U.S. visitors would do well to copy this by clearly expressing thanks and by repeating these expressions at least several times.**

---

* NOTE: In case the reader is wondering, it is true that tourists from the United States would do well to avoid tap water in Mexico. A wise alternative would be to drink bottled water, called aqua mineral, which is available at almost any restaurant. When visiting someone's home, one can request bottled water; however, when a glass of tap water is offered or used in mixed drinks it is, of course, rude to refuse it or request that the drink be made over again with different water. (Remember that the ice in a drink is made of water. While one obviously knows this, many tourists simply overlook this fact.) A way to avoid this problem is to ask for drinks without ice.

** NOTE: Compliments on a host's house and appearance are, of course, always welcome. Male guests, however, should avoid complimenting the appearance of a host's wife. Well-intentioned compliments of this kind can very easily be misinterpreted by one's host whose sensibility to such comments may be quite different from those of a visitor from the U.S. Likewise if one is bringing or sending flowers before or after a social engagement, male guests would do well to address the flowers to the entire family. Or if flowers are sent directly to the hostess, then they should be addressed to her *y familia* (and family), to avoid any possible misconception that a male guest is sending the flowers only to her.

11. When a Mexican extends an invitation to dinner at a restaurant, it does not necessarily mean that he plans to pay for the meal.

When the guest wants to pay for both meals, simply offering to pay is usually not enough. The guest must insist many times, not just once, otherwise the invitation will not be taken seriously.

12. U.S. visitors will often make believe that they like a local specialty which is served to them in someone's home.

They believe that if they do not eat certain foods at all, they take the risk of insulting their hosts. Actually, this can be a dangerous social route to take. A better approach might be to highly praise the food that one likes and that agrees with one's palate, and completely avoid the food that does not appear appetizing. This way it will appear as though one forgot the other food or that one is so full after eating the other food which s/he has proclaimed delicious, that s/he has not "worked" his/her way to the other offerings.

No one is expected to eat everything, and a guest can communicate dislike for a local food with the eyes and with facial expression, just as well as with words. Leaving a plate half empty is a statement in itself, and the hostess is liable to be more attentive to the reactions of visitors than she is to the reactions of locals. Unfortunately, the conclusion she may arrive at is that Americans feel superior to Mexicans and do not want to eat their food.

A very dangerous assumption on the part of U.S. visitors is that their host's maid prepared their food, and a real or implied criticism of the food will not really matter to the hosts. Nothing is further from the truth.

Additionally, it is unwise to show too great a concern over possible food contamination. The information and misinformation about the level of sanitation in Latin American can lead to unreasonable fears on the part of travelers. A few years ago one foreign visitor at a Mexican resort was so afraid of the local food that she refused all solid food and only drank liquids. She eventually became so weak that she had to be taken to the local hospital as an emergency patient.

It is true, however, that levels of sanitation can vary greatly from country to country and though some U.S. visitors feel that just about anything they eat in Latin America can cause food poisoning or "Montezuma's Revenge," this is an over-statement.

Well-cooked food presents no problem. For short-term visitors, uncooked vegetables and salads should be avoided. Armed with this knowledge a visitor from the United States can make intelligent choices and simply leave certain foods off the menu, which is perfectly legitimate, and can do so without making a big fuss. After all, not everybody eats everything and everyone has personal tastes and preferences in food.

When asked beforehand about what type of food would be preferred for a dinner party, the U.S. visitor would be wise to leave the actual selection of food to the host. Unfortunately, U.S. visitors are often completely unaware of the relative cost of food items in Mexico and they have been known to select foods that are very common and inexpensive in the United States, only to learn that these same foods are really delicacies in Mexico. Purchases of these items can imply a cost that can be a real burden for a middle-class family in Mexico. For example, one U.S. citizen visiting Mexico showed his marked preference for fresh pineapples, reasoning that Mexico was partly a tropical country and was a great producer of pineapples which therefore must be very cheap. He was greatly surprised to find that in certain neighborhood stores where he was living, this fruit was as expensive if not more expensive than he usually found it to be in the United States. Those who have not visited Mexico recently may be surprised to find that this situation also pertains to a whole host of consumer items including gasoline, despite the fact that Mexico is the world's fourth largest producer of oil.

SOCIAL MINE FIELDS
(OR WHAT NOT TO DO WHEN SOCIALIZING IN MEXICO)

1. One should never criticize or even joke about the local food or wine.
2. Sandals and/or shorts are not worn by adults except in tropical climates. Men should wear shirts and ties of a conservative character.

3. One must not be loud. Use of a moderate tone of voice is important. Also one must not dominate the conversation, but be a good listener. Being on new ground, one will find s/he has a lot to learn.

4. When an invited guest, one should not forget to say "thank you" loud and clear, and a number of times. This is an expression that is hard to overdo in Mexico.

5. One should get to know the local currency and never refer to it in derogatory terms such as, "How much is this worth in real money?"

6. Latin Americans like to drink a lot of coffee. Mexicans like to drink it black and very strong. One should not refuse coffee when it is offered, even if it is not to one's taste. Such a refusal can be interpreted as a social slight against a Mexican concept of hospitality.

7. One must never chew with one's mouth open, or even partially open.

8. The etiquette of table setting for formal dinners is especially important in Mexico. To mistake one utensil for another is a real faux pas.

   The dessert fork is found above the plate. The salad fork is inside the meat fork. When the salad is served first, the salad fork is the first fork in the setting. There is usually one knife for the appetizer and a larger knife for the meat. Soup spoons can be found to the right of the knives.

9. One must not slam knives or forks on the table, nor toss them carelessly onto a table. Mexicans are sensitive to such gestures.

10. It is important to avoid talking about controversial subjects such as politics if one's knowledge of Mexico is limited to what was read in the newspapers or printed in popular news magazines such as *Time* and *Newsweek*. Mexicans feel that U.S. views of Latin America are largely based on false stereotypes and distortions that are frequently presented in the popular press. To repeat a notion such as "Mexico is a wonderful country. It is too bad that its presidents haven't been helping the U.S. in its war on drugs as much as they might have," will leave Mexican colleagues bristling, ready to re-

ply that it is the U.S. creating the problem with its monstrous consumption of drugs.*

On the other hand, a guaranteed way to make a very good impression on Mexican business partners is to do one's homework beforehand and mention appreciation of local landmarks, museums, parks, works of art, and so forth, or to demonstrate knowledge and appreciation of the latest shows, movies, and books that are popular in Mexico.

Even a passing comment on events from Mexican history will impress Mexican associates since people from the U.S. have the reputation of wearing cultural blinders and of being completely oblivious to historical events of other countries, especially those of Latin America. (Even worse, people from the U.S. have the international reputation of being ahistorical, not even having an interest or knowledge of their own history, let alone that of another country.)

One must not make the mistake of thinking that everything from the so-called "Spanish" world is one and the same. There are great differences between the countries of Latin America and Spain, so just mentioning some of the books from Spain that were read as part of a high school or college Spanish course will not do the trick. One should realize that the Mexicans have a love-hate relationship with Spain and Spaniards are still sometimes referred to in Mexico derogatorily as, *Los gachupines.*

11. Likewise, one should not automatically take offense, or frown during the dinner conversation if one hears U.S. visitors or even oneself referred to as *gringo*. The term is not necessarily derogatory. Meaning depends on the tone of voice and the context.

12. It is very important that one call a Mexican business colleague at the office to confirm an invitation, *not* at home.

---

* NOTE: Readers may be smiling as they read this, thinking that they would never fall into this type of trap. Perhaps that is so, but conversations can take strange twists and turns and the animated nature of many discussions often lead people to make statements that they never thought they would make. Naturally, this is especially true when alcoholic drinks are present at a social event.

13. When acting as a guest one may find that toasts are common. It is better form to allow your host to give his toast before the guest gives his/her own.

14. When introducing U.S. diplomats in Mexico be sure to include the words "of the United States of America," after the title to avoid saying he or she is from or is representing the "American embassy" or is representing "the American government." It is important to keep in mind that all citizens of the Western Hemisphere are Americans.

15. If U.S. visitors are attending a social event with high school or college-aged children, they must be aware that very informal, not to say ragged dress, often associated with the student/youth subculture in the United States, will most likely be interpreted by Mexicans as representing poverty and a general lack of culture. Straggly and unkempt hair and poor looking dress may make your hosts wonder if the people they invited are really the kind of people they wish to associate with, either socially or professionally.

16. One should always put him/herself in his/her host's place. It will then be easier to understand why Mexicans are supersensitive to slights and negative comparisons. If any opinions are made on the local cuisine, wine, or even soft drinks and coffee, you would be wise to keep them silent unless one thinks the Mexican offering happens to be preferable to the U.S. counterpart.

17. If one disagrees with the host, it must be done amicably. U.S. businesspeople are in the habit of asking a lot of questions early in a relationship, about their conversation partners: how much they earn, their working hours, and the kind of neighborhood they live in. This type of "interrogation," often so much a part of habitual social behavior, can be interpreted as impolite and intrusive.

A CLOSING NOTE

Finally, one should remember that any social expression of kindliness, warmth, and acceptance that one would wish to be shown to oneself as a host, should be extended to one's own host in double or triple amounts. The Latin culture is a highly expressive one and U.S. manners are on display and are the object of special scrutiny.

For example, when one is saying thank you for a dinner party, one should do so profusely and repeatedly. When saying goodbye, one should try to add some personal note of thanks and appreciation along with more obvious comments.

The road to social acceptability is composed not only of special items of information such as the ones outlined above, but is also made of the proper expression of a positive and accepting attitude which displays the realization that we all have a lot to learn from each other, both individually and nationally in terms of culture and standards of conduct.

Appendix

Holidays

While Indian and Catholic holidays are both celebrated in Mexico and, depending on the region of the country, different holidays receive greater or less importance and are celebrated on different dates, all regions, north or south, east or west, rural or urban, celebrate the Virgin of Guadalupe, probably best described as Mexico's patron saint.

The story is an elaborate one. Shortly after the Spanish conquest, Fray (Father) Juan de Zumárraga, the first Archbishop of Mexico, ordered the destruction of all important pagan deities and shrines. The one with the widest cult near the capital was the Aztec goddess of earth and corn, Tonantzin. The natives mourned the loss so deeply that, as the story goes, the native-looking Virgin of Guadalupe was sent to take her place.

Early one morning a poor peasant, who was a recent convert, was on his way to the Franciscan church at Tlalteloco to receive instruction. As he crossed Tepeyac Hill near where Tonantzin's shrine had been, he heard heavenly music and a sweet voice calling his name. There he saw the Virgin with her feet resting on a rock bed that gleamed like precious jewels. She told him to ask the Bishop for a church to be built at that spot so that she could protect and love the people, "For I am the mother of all of you who dwell in this land."

Juan Diego, the Indian, tried to see the Bishop and could not and when he returned to the hill to report to the Virgin, awaiting him, he reported his lack of success and told her she would have to find a more worthy messenger. She insisted that he try again. Juan Diego had better success reaching the Bishop this time, but little success getting permission for the church to be built. However, he did raise the Bishop's curiosity and after asking that Juan return with some divine sign, the Bishop sent a member of the household to follow

Juan Diego. The tracker lost the Indian in the hills and told the Bishop to punish Juan for telling tales. In the meantime, Juan was meeting with the Virgin who made arrangements to give him a sign for his next meeting.

The Virgin instructed Juan Diego to pick flowers from the rock on which she rested her feet and carry them, secretly, in his cape, showing them only to the Bishop. After a bit of trouble reaching the Bishop, Juan was finally successful and, upon opening his cape, a carpet of roses fell out leaving an apparition of the Virgin showing on the cape. The Bishop was convinced, fell to his knees, and begged forgiveness. He placed Juan's cape over the altar and asked him to instruct him as to where the church was to be built.

The shrine is the holiest in Mexico and it is a dream of good Catholic Mexicans to visit this mecca. Along with those who are healthy, the sick, the blind, and the lame come to drink the water at the shrine. It is said that if a stranger drinks there s/he will return to Mexico.

The anniversary of Juan Diego's first encounter with the Virgin is December 12. Many crawl on their knees a mile or more to visit the shrine on this day. It is customary to walk the distance of the fourteen stations of the cross there on December 11.

Other customs include the blessing of seeds in the churches on Candlemas Day, February 2. At the planting, crosses are set up in the fields and blessed with holy water, prayers, offerings of candles, and incense.

Harvest time brings thanksgiving fiestas at churches. On haciendas, owners traditionally give fiestas to workers that include food, drink, music, and dance.

When rain is needed, the image of miraculous saints are taken out and carried in a procession complete with flowers, lighted candles, and lighted censers. Fireworks are shot off to produce rainclouds. San Isidoro is the patron saint of the farmers and masses are said, before and after these processions. Oxen are used to pull decorated ploughs.

Days of important saints are considered good for planting. May 3, the Day of the Holy Cross, is also considered a good planting day.

Finally, it is important to remember that from Christmas to the third of January and during the Holy Week until Easter, most Mexicans are on vacation. Therefore, a lot of offices, shops, and services will have limited hours and personnel during these holidays.

IMPORTANT MEXICAN HOLIDAYS

Only nationwide holidays, during which offices and shops close, are provided here. Businesspeople should make sure to check any local area they are visiting or working in for regional holidays.

Holiday	*Date*
New Year	January 1
Los Reyes Magos (Epiphany) (present receiving time for children)	January 6
Constitution Day	February 5
Benito Juarez's Birthday	March 21
Holy Week (Semana Santa), Easter	

(Passion is dramatized. Thursday is saved for the last supper and the arrest of Christ. Friday morning is for the sentence and procession, afternoon is for crucifixion and descent from the cross. Saturday morning is the Mass of Glory. Easter Sunday, by comparison, is relatively tame.)

Labor Day	May 1
Battle of Puebla (anniversary of the Battle over the French 1862)	May 5
President's Annual Address to the Nation	September 1
Independence Day	September 16
Virgin and Fiesta of Zapopan	October 4, 5
Columbus Day	October 12
Day of the Dead	November 2
Anniversary of the Revolution	November 20
Virgin of Guadalupe Day	December 12, ending as late as the 18th
Christmas	December 25

Glossary

Spanish vowels:
> a = father
> e = met
> i = ee/meet
> o = toe
> u = oo/food
> y = (when a vowel) like i

Spanish consonants:
> cu followed by a vowel = kw
> g followed by i or e + j is aspirated
> h = ch/bach
> h = silent (the only silent letter)
> hu followed by a vowel = w
> j is like the English h
> ll = y in English (consonant)
> qu = k
> r = thread
> rr is trilled

Aztec:
> tl as in atlas, not Spanish or English *tel*
> x and j interchanged and pronounced the same
> some x = sh
> some x = s
> Other Indian pronunciations:
>> Coaixtlahuacán = koh-ah-eesh-tla-wah'-kan
>> Cuauhtitlán = kwow-tee-tlahn'
>> Huichol = wee-chol'
>> Jicaque = hee-kah'-kay

Mixtec = mees'-tek
Oaxaca = wah-hah'-kah
Quetzalcoatl = kets-al-koh'-atl
Xut = shoot

BASIC BUSINESS VOCABULARY

acciones   stocks

acreditar   to credit

activos   assets

adjunto   enclosed

administración de negocios   business management

administrador(a)   administrator

aduana   customs

ahorrar   to save

ajuste   adjustment

alquilar   to rent

anular   to write off, to void

apartado postal   post-office box

apoderado   empowered, proxy, attorney, agent

apoyo de precios   price support

arancel   tariff

arancel de aduana   customs tariff

arriendo   a lease

auditor   auditor

automatización   automation

aval   endorsement

balance   balance sheet

balanza comercial   trade balance

balanza de pagos   balance of payments

banca   banking, banks in general

bancarrota   bankrupt

banco de ahorros   savings bank

barata   a sale (reduced price)

barato   cheap

bienes   goods

bienes de capital   capital goods

bienes de consumo   consumer goods

bienes raíces   real estate

bienes y servicios   goods and services

boicot   boycott

bolsa   stock exchange

bono   bond

buque de vapor   steam ship

caja   box, cash register

cajero(a)   cashier

caja de seguridad   safe deposit box

calcular   to calculate

cambio   change

camión   truck

canjear   to exchange

capital (el)   capital (money)

capital (la)   capital city

cargo   charge, debit

cargos por concepto de manejo   handling charges

caro   expense

carta de crédito   letter of credit

casa de moneda   mint

circulante   money in circulation

clave   code or key

clientela   clientele

colección   collection

comanditario   silent partner

comerciante (el or **la)** businessperson

comercio business, commerce

comisión commission

compra purchase

comprar a plazos to buy on time

computadora computer

consignación consignment

contador accountant

contratista contractor

convenio agreement

corredor broker, stock broker

corredor de aduana customs broker

correo mail

corresponsal correspondent

costo expense, cost

costos fijos fixed costs

cotización quotation

cotizar to quote (prices)

cuenta account

cuenta corriente checking account

cuenta de ahorros   savings account

cheque   check

cheque de viajeros   traveler's check

dato   fact

decomisar   to confiscate

defectuoso   defective

demanda   demand

dependiente   clerk

depósitos a plazo   time deposits

derecho   right, law

derecho aduanal   customs duties

derechos de exportación   export duties

desarrollo   development

descuento   discount

desembolso   disbursement

desgaste   wear (as of machinery)

despacho   office

destinatario   addressee

deuda   debt

deudor   debtor

día hábil   business day

dinero   money

dirección   address

dividendo   dividend

divisa   foreign exchange

economía   economy

economizar   economize

efectivo   cash

embarque   shipment

empacar   to pack

empresario   entrepreneur

endosar   to endorse

entrega   delivery

entrega futura   forward delivery

entrevista   interview

enviar   to send

envío   the mailing

envolver   to wrap up

escaso   scarce

escrito   in writing

etiqueta   label

exportación   export

extranjero   foreigner

fábrica   factory

fabricante   manufacturer

fabricar   to make, manufacture

factura   invoice

fecha de cierre   closing date

fidecomiso   trust

fijo   fixed

financiar   to finance

firmar   to sign

fondo   fund

franqueo   postage

franquicia   franchise

furgón   freight car

galón   gallon

ganado   cattle

ganancia   earnings, profit

ganar   to earn

ganga bargain

garantía guarantee

garantizar to guarantee

gastar to spend

gasto expense

gerencia management

giro money order

gráfica chart

gravamen lien

hierro iron

hipoteca mortgage

hoja piece of paper

horario schedule

horario diario daily schedule

huelga strike

importe amount

impuesto tax

informe report

ingeniero engineer

ingreso income

instalar   to install

inventarios   inventories

inversión   investment

investigación   research

jefe (masc.), **jefa** (fem.)   boss

junta   board, council

jurado   jury

kilo   kilogram

kilómetro   kilometer

labor   work

lema   slogan

letrero   sign

libra   pound

licencia   license

límite de crédito   credit limit

línea   line

liquidación   liquidation sale

llamada   call

llamada de larga distancia   long distance call

llamada por cobrar   collect call

llegar   to arrive

máquina   machine

maquinista   machinist

marca   brand

materia   matter, material

mayorista   wholesaler

mecanógrafo/a (fem.)   typist

medir   measure

mejorar   to improve

membrete   letterhead

menorista   retailer

mercado   market

mercadotécnia   marketing

mercancía   merchandise

moneda   money, coin

muestra   sample

multa   fine

negociar   to negotiate

negocio   business

neto   net

nivel   level

nombrar   to name, appoint

noticia   news

oficina   office

ofrecimiento   offering

oportunidad   opportunity

ordenar   to order

otorgar   to hand over, grant, execute

pacto   agreement

pagaré   promissory note, I.O.U.

papel   paper, role

paro   strike

pautas   guidelines

pedido   order

pérdida   loss

peso   weight

planificación   planning

plazo   term, time

(comprar a) plazo   buy on time

por mayor   wholesale

por menor retail

precio price

precio de costo cost price

préstamo loan

prima premium

promedio average

presupuesto budget

propina tip

prórroga delay

prueba proof

puerto port

quiebra breakage, bankruptcy

rapidez speed

recargo overcharge

recibo receipt

reclamo claim

recursos resources

red net, network

redactar to edit

remate auction, sale

renta   income, rent

requisitos   requirements

riesgo   risk

romper   to break

rompimiento   breakage

salario   wages

saldar   to settle a debt

saldo   balance

seguridad   safety

seguros   insurance

sindicato   union

sobregiro   overdraft

sociedad anónima   corporation

socio   partner

solicitar   to apply, request

subsidio   subsidy

superávit   surplus

taller   workshop

talón   check stub

tanda   shift

tarjeta   card

tasa   rate

tela   cloth, fabric

telefonear   to call on the phone

término   term

testigo   witness

título   title

traspaso   assignment

tratado   treaty

tratar   to treat, deal with, try

usura   usury

usurero   usurer

valer   to be worth

vencimiento   maturity (as of securities)

ventaja   advantage

verificar   to verify

vivienda   housing

SOME GENERAL VOCABULARY

abrazo (ah-brahs'-oh): a greeting consisting of approximately two hearty backslaps accompanying a handshake

aguardiente (ah-gwahr-dee-ehn'-teh): brandy or liquor

ahijado (ah-ee-hah'-doh): godchild *(fem.* ahijada*)*

alberca (al-bear-ka) pool

ancianos (ahn-see-ah'-nohs): old men; highly respected village elders

antojitos (ahn-toh-hee'-tos): popular Mexican dishes

arras (ah'-rrahs): 13 pieces of silver the groom slips into the hands of the bride during the marriage ceremony in the Catholic church

atole (ah-toh'-leh): cornmeal gruel, sometimes flavored with chocolate

autoridades (aw-toh-ree-dah'-dehs): authorities; judges in a bullfight

barrio (bah-ree'-oh): a neighborhood of a city/town, usually with a church and plaza of its own

CANACINTRA (National Chamber of Processing Industries): a major employers' organization

CONCAMIN (Confederation of Industrial Chambers): a major employers' organization

CTM (Confederation of Mexican Workers): the country's main labor organization

cacique (kah-see'-heh): chief; leader

camisa (kah-mee'-sah): shirt (term applies to a *camisa* worn by either sex)

canastas (kah-nahs'-tahs): baskets

cantinas (kahn-tee'-nahs): saloons

chamarra (chah-mah'-rrah): man's short jacket, made of wool or leather

chaparro (cha-par-o) short person

charros (chah'-rrohs): Mexican horseback riders who do cowboy tricks (fem. *charrras*)

chicha (chee'-chah): ritual sugar-cane brandy of the Highlands (Chiapas); soft drink made of chia seeds

chilango (chee-lahn'-goh): a mestizo resident of the Central Highlands

chingadazo (cheen-gah-dah'-szo): a heavy physical blow

chingadera (cheen-gah-deh'-rah): dirty talk

chirimoya (chee-ree-moh'-yah): tropical fruit with soft, pulpy flesh around a big stone that is green outside

coleta (koh-leh'-tah): false braid worn by a bullfighter

compadrazgo (kohm-pah-drahs'-go): godparenthood

compadres (kohm-pah'-dres): persons related through godparenthood

copitas (koh-pee'-tas): cups; drinks

costumbre (kohs-toom'-breh): customs

coyotes (koh-yoh-tes): daring individuals who guide illegal migration, generally for profit

cuadrilla (kwah-dree'-ya): a crew; bullfighter's helpers

curandera (koo-rahn'-deh'-rah): medicine woman (masc. *currandero*)

dueño (dwehn'-yo): owner

ejidos (eh-hee'-dohs): small cooperative farms, derived from government-seized agricultural tracts, that were given to peasant farmers

enredo (ehn-reh'-doh): misunderstanding

FDN (National Democratic Front): a national political party

fandango (fahn-dahn'-goh): dance; a party

fayuca (fah-yoo'-kah): contraband

ferias (feh'-ree-ahs): combination fairs and religious fiestas

fronterizos (frohn-teh'-ree-zohs): individuals living in border cities

guajolote (gwah-hoo-loh'-teh): turkey

guayabera (gwi-ah-beh'-rah): man's white, summer shirt

güero (wear-o): blond

guitarra (guee-tah'-rrah): guitar

hacendado (ah-sehn-dah'-do): owner of a large estate (*hacienda*)

huipil (wee-peel'): straight, sleeveless, shapeless blouse

indito (een-dee'-toh): little Indian man (used in affection or contempt, depending on how it is said and by and to whom)

jamaica (hah-mah-ee'-hah): soft drink made from jamaica flowers

jarocho (har-ok'-koh): locals of the Veracruz region

jefe (heh'-feh): chief; boss

jorongo (hoh-rohn'-goh): medium-sized sarape, generally worn folded over the shoulder or open overhead

juegos (hweh'-gohs): games

juez (hwehs): judge

licenciado (lee-sehn-see-ah'-doh): college graduate (**El licenciado**: professional title, lawyer)

madre (mah'-dreh): mother

madrina (mah-dree'-nah): godmother

maestro (mah-es'-troh): teacher, honorific title

mande (man day'): What?

masa (mah'-sah): corn dough for tortillas

maquiladora, maquila (mah-kee-ah-doh'-rah): nickname for the Border Industrialization Program (PIF) which allows U.S. companies to assemble products in Mexico for reexport; a company taking part in the PIF

me vale madre (meh vah'-leh mah'-dreh): lit. it's worth mother to me, used as a vulgarity for I don't give a damn

mero (meh'-roh): the chief one

mesero (mas-ero'): waiter

mestiza (mehs-tee'-sah): woman of mixed Indian and Spanish blood (masc. *mestizo*)

mexicanos (meh-hee-kah'-nos): Mexicans; natives' designation for city people

mezcal (mehs-kahl'): intoxicating drink of Oaxaca, fermented from maguey hearts

mi hijo (mee hee'-oh): my son, used as term of endearment for husband

mole (Aztec *molli*) (moh'-leh): piquant sauce for meats and fowl

mole de olla (moh'-leh del oh'-ya): beef with red chili sauce

morrales (moh-rrah'-les): bags

muleta (moo-leh'-tah): small red cape used by a bullfighter

muy padre (mwee pah'-dreh): excellent

NAFTA (North American Free Trade Agreement): a trilateral trade agreement currently being negotiated between Mexico, the United States, and Canada

ni modo (nee moh'-doh): tough luck

norteños (nor-ten'-yohs): northerners

Oaxaqueños (oh-ah-ha-kehn'-yohs): persons living in Oaxaca

PAN (National Action Party): a leading political party, principally competitive with PRI

PDM (Mexican Democratic Party): a national political party

PRI (pree): the Institutional Revolutionary Party, the country's largest political party, which has dominated national politics for over fifty years

PRT (Workers Revolutionary Party): a national political party

padre/el padre (pah-dreh): father; father figure

padrino (pah-dree'-noh): godfather

papito (pah-pee'-toh): little father, used as term of endearment from mother to young son

pascua (pahs'-kwah): Pentecost

pelado (peh-lah'-doh): literal: plucked, bare, peeled, treeless, husked, penniless; figurative: poor, bare soul, one of the lowest social character, generally urban

peones (peh-oh'-nehs): those helping the bullfighter in the ring; an unskilled, poorly paid worker

pepitas (peh-pee'-tahs): melon seeds

peyote (pey-yoh'-teh): sacred little cactus plants of Tarahumaras and Huichols

piloncillo (pee-lohn'-see'-yoh): brown sugar

piñata (peen-yah'-tah): clay jar filled with sweets and toys; covered papier-mache figure, broken by someone in a blindfold during the posada fiestas

pinole (pee-noh'-leh): powder of toasted corn, eaten dry or mixed with water

pobrecitos (poh-breh-see'-tohs): poor things

porra (poh'-rrah): gangs of fans at a bullfight

posadas (poh-sah'-dahs): lodging, applied to Christmas fiestas that dramatize Mary and Joseph's journey to Bethlehem and asking for lodging along the way

pozole (poh-soh'-leh): corn dough; a native food (Jalisco: a dish with pork and chickpeas)

pulque (pool'-keh): brewed from juice of the maguey plant

puros (poo'-rohs): cigars

quesadillas (kehs-ah-dee'-yahs): turnovers, fried in lard and filled with cheese, beans, potatoes, etc.

quexquemetl (qehsh-keh-mehtl'): cape-like blouse without sleeves

red (rehd): net for fishing or a net formed into a bag

refrescos (reh-frehs'-kos): soft drinks

regiomontanos (reh-hee-oh-mohn'-tah-nohs): inhabitants of the Monterrey region

rodete (roh-deh'-teh): hair formed into a roll with strands of wool

rollo (roh'-yo): shirt of many yards of cloth, laid in pleats around the waist

sarape (sah-rah'-peh): blanket

sinfonía (seen-foh-nee'-ah): symphony; musical introduction played by the mariachis before each song

soldadera (sohl-dah-deh'-rah): woman soldier who follows her man to battle

soldado (sohl-dah'-doh): soldier

suerte (swehr'-teh): stunt or trick

tacos (tah'-kohs): sandwiches with meat, cheese, and other fillings wrapped in a tortilla

tamarindo (tah-mah-reen'-dah): soft drink made with seeds of tamarind trees

tapatío (tah-pah'-tee-koh): a native of the Guadalajara region

tapetes (teh-peh'-tehs): rugs or carpets

tepache (teh-pah'-cheh): soft drink made with pineapple, turned into a hard drink by fermentation or mixing with pulque

tequila (teh-kee'-lah): alcoholic drink from a small agave plant (Jalisco)

tianguis (tee angees) native market

tostadas (tohs-tah'-dos): tortillas, deep fried and covered with meat, etc.

trago (trah'-goh): a swallow; in Chiapas, intoxicating drinks

tuba (too'-bah): soft drink made from the sap of the coconut palms

tunas (too'-nahs): prickly-pear fruit

tzotzil (tsoh'-tseel'): indigenous language of Chiapas

una madre (oo'-nah mah'-dreh): slang for something unimportant

un desmadre (oon dehs mah'-dreh): slang: chaos

vacilada (vah-see-lah'-dah): literal: vacillation; slang: a laugh with the tongue in cheek; good times

vaquero (vah-keh'-roh): herdsman, cowboy

vecinos (veh-see'-nohs): neighbors (used by natives when speaking of citified people)

velador (veh-la-dohr'): watchman

veladora (veh-la-doh'-rah): light that is always lighted on the alter

Yucatecos (yoo-kah-teh'-cohs): natives of the Yucatán region

Yuntzilob (yoon-tseel-ob): Mayan saints referred to as little people made of air

Bibliography

Adler, N. J. and J. Graham. Fall 1989. "Cross-Cultural Interaction: The International Comparison Fallacy." *Journal of International Business*. 515-527.

Baldridge, L. 1978. *The Amy Vanderbilt Complete Book of Etiquette Revised and Expanded by Letitia Baldridge*. Garden City, NY: Doubleday and Co.

Bank of Mexico. S.A. *Annual Report*.

Bell, D. September 9, 1975. "The Clock Watchers." *Time*. 55-57.

Boseman, F. G. and A. Phatak. 1978. "Management Practices of Industrial Enterprises in Mexico: A Comparative Study." *International Management Review*. 78:43-49.

Bureau of Mines. 1989. "U.S. Environment Programme." *Environmental Data Report*. Cambridge: U.S. Department of the Interior.

"Economic Trends Report." February 1987. Mexico City: U.S. Embassy.

Fisher, G. 1980. *International Negotiation: A Cross-Cultural Perspective*. Chicago: The Intercultural Press.

Geography on File. 1991. New York: Facts on File.

Gonzalez, A. and P. G. Zimbarlo. March 1985. "Time in Perspective." *Psychology Today*. 21.

Gordon, J. G. 1985. *Good Neighbors: Communicating with the Mexicans*. Yarmouth, ME: The Intercultural Press.

Hall, E. T. 1987. *Hidden Differences*. Garden City, NY: Doubleday Books.

Hendon, D. W. and R. Hendon. 1990. *World-Class Negotiation*. New York: John Wiley and Sons.

Hunter, B. (ed.) 1992. *The Statesman's Yearbook*. 129th edition. 1992-93. New York: St. Martin's Press.

International Business Research. *Market Estimates*. Washington, DC: U.S. Department of Commerce.

International Finance Corporation. 1990. *Emerging Stockmarkets Factbook*. Washington DC: International Finance Corporation.

Jankowic, E. and S. Bernstein. 1986. *Behave Yourself! The Working Guide to Business Etiquette.* Englewood Cliffs, NJ: Prentice Hall.

Kagan, S. and G. D. Knight. December 1979. "Cooperation-Cooperation and Self-Esteem: A Case of Cross Cultural Psychology." *Journal of Cross-Cultural Psychology.* 1:454-467.

Morales, J. S. M. 1985. *100 Preguntas y respuestas en torno a la economia mexicana.* Mexico City: Editorial Oceano.

Pastor, R. A. and J. G. Castaneda. 1988. *Limits to Friendship: The United States and Mexico.* New York: Alfred A. Knopf.

Paz, O. 1986. *El laberinto de la soledad.* Mexico City: Fondo de Cultural Económica.

Rama, C. M. 1975. *La imagen de los Estados Unidos en La América Latina de Simón Bolívar a Allende.* Mexico City: Sepsetenta.

Riding, A. 1985. *Distant Neighbors: A Portrait of the Mexicans.* New York: Alfred A. Knopf.

Ruiz, R. E. 1992. *Truimphs and Tragedy: A History of the Mexican People.* New York: W.W. Norton and Co.

Twin Plant News. 1991. El Paso, Tx.

Valdivieso, J. H. and L. T. Valdivieso. 1988. *Negocios y comunicaciones.* Lexington, MA: D.C. Heath and Co.

Vázquez, Josephine Zoraida. 1976. *Historia General de México.* El Colegio de Mexico.

Weintraub, S. 1984. *Free Trade Between Mexico and the United States.* Washington, DC: Brookings.

_____ 1990. *Marriage of Convenience: Relations Between Mexico and the United States.* New York: Oxford University Press.

Whatley, A. 1985. *Managing in Mexico.* Las Cruces, NM: The Border Institute.

Whatley, A. and L. Kelley. July 1986. "The American Manager in Mexico: A Managerial Dilemma." *Massey Journal of Asian and Pacific Business*, (New Zealand). 2, 2.

Whatley, A. and E. Kraus. June 1990. "Using Organization Development Technology in Mexico: Issues and Problems." *International Journal of Management.* 7, 2.

World Fact Book. 1991. Washington, DC: CIA.

World Resources Institute. 1993. *Information Please Environmental Almanac.* Boston: Houghton Mifflin.

Additional Sources of Information
on Business Protocol and Working in Mexico

The following is a list of information sources on conducting business in Mexico. While this list is not all-inclusive, it is intended to provide additional perspective and insight into Mexican culture and business practices.

BOOKS

Adler, Nancy J. 1991. *International Dimensions of Organizational Behavior.* Boston: PWS-Kent Publishing Co.

Axtell, Roger E. 1985. (editor and compiler). *Do's and Taboos Around the World.* Elmsford, NY: The Benjamin Company.

Camp, Roderic A. (editor). 1986. *Mexico's Political Stability: The Next Five Years.* Boulder, CO: Westview Press.

Chesanow, Neil. 1991. *The World Class Executive, How to Do Business Like a Pro Around the World.* New York: Rawson Associates.

Copeland, Lennie and Lewis Griggs. 1985. *Going International.* New York: Random House.

Fisher, Glen. 1980. *International Negotiation, A Cross-Cultural Perspective.* Chicago: The Intercultural Press.

Gorden, Raymond L. 1990. *Living in Latin America, A Case Study in Cross-Cultural Communication.* Chicago: National Textbook Company.

Gordon, John G. 1985. *Good Neighbors, Communicating With the Mexicans.* Yarmouth, ME: The Intercultural Press.

Grayson, George W. 1988. *Oil and Mexican Foreign Policy.* Pittsburgh: University of Pittsburgh Press.

Greenberg, James B. 1989. *Blood Ties: Life and Violence in Rural Mexico.* Tucson: University of Arizona Press.

Griffin, Trenholme J. and W. Russel Daggatt. 1990. *The Global Negotiator.* New York: Harper Business Publishing.

Hall, Edward T. 1969. *The Hidden Dimension.* Garden City, NY: Doubleday Books.

Hall, Edward T. and Mildred Reed Hall. 1987. *Hidden Differences.* Garden City, NY: Anchor Press/Doubleday Books.

Harris, Philip R. and Robert T. Moran. 1979. *Managing Cultural Differences*. Houston: Gulf Publishing Co.

Hendon, Donald W. and Rebecca Hendon. 1990. *World-Class Negotiation*. New York: John Wiley and Sons.

Herring, Hubert. 1959. *A History of Latin America from the Beginning to the Present*. New York: Alfred A. Knopf.

Hofstede, Gert. 1984. *Culture's Consequences*. Beverly Hills: Sage Publishing.

Jarvis, Ana C. and Luis Lebredo. 1992. *Spanish for Business and Finance*. Lexington, MA: D.C. Heath and Co.

Koopman, Albert. 1991. *Transcultural Management*. Cambridge, MA: Basil Blackwell.

Koopman, Albert. 1991. *Transnational Management*. Cambridge, MA: Basil Blackwell.

Noble, Judith and Jaime Lacasa. 1991. *The Hispanic Way*. Chicago: Passport Books.

Pastor, Robert A. and Jorge G. Castaneda. 1988. *Limits to Friendship: The United States and Mexico*. New York: Alfred A. Knopf.

Phatak, Arvind V. 1992. *International Dimensions of Management*. Boston: PWS-Kent Publishing Co.

Riding, Alan. 1985. *Distant Neighbors: A Portrait of the Mexicans*. New York: Alfred A. Knopf.

Ruiz, Ramon Eduardo. 1992. *Triumphs and Tragedy: A History of the Mexican People*. New York: W.W. Norton and Co.

Ryans, John K. Jr. and James C. Baker. 1967. *World Marketing, A Multinational Approach*. New York: John Wiley and Sons.

Simpson, Lesley Byrd. 1959. *Many Mexicos*. Berkeley: University of California Press.

Terpstra, Vern. 1988. *International Dimensions of Marketing*. Boston: PWS-Kent Publishing.

Weintraub, Sidney. 1984. *Free Trade Between Mexico and the United States*. Washington, DC: Brookings Institute.

Weintraub, Sidney. 1990. *Marriage of Convenience: Relations between Mexico and the United States*. New York: Oxford University Press.

Whatley, Arthur. 1985. *Managing in Mexico*. Las Cruces, NM: The Border Institute.

ARTICLES

Adler, Nancy J. and J. Graham. Fall 1989. "Cross-Cultural Interaction: The International Comparison Fallacy," *Journal of International Business.* 515-527.

Bell, Daniel. September 9, 1975. "The Clock Watchers," *Time.* 55-57.

Belli, Pedro. July-August 1991. "Globalizing the Rest of the World," *Harvard Business Review.* 50-55.

Boseman, F. Glenn and Arvind Phatak. 1978. "Management Practices of Industrial Enterprises in Mexico: A Comparative Study," *International Management Review.* 78, 1:43-49.

Fadiman, Jeffrey A. July-August 1986. "A Traveler's Guide to Gifts and Bribes," *Harvard Business Review.* 122-131.

Ferrari, Sergio. 1977. "A Mexican Approach to Industrial Training," *Industrial Management Review.* 17, 4:82-88.

Gonzalez, Alexander and Philip G. Zimbarlo. March 1985. "Time in Perspective," *Psychology Today.* 21.

Kagan, S. and George D. Knight. December 1979. "Cooperation-Cooperation and Self-Esteem, A Case of Cross Cultural Psychology," *Journal of Cross-Cultural Psychology.* 1, 4:454-467.

Ross, Robert. October-November 1991. "The Human Factor," *North/South.* 46-48.

Whatley, Arthur and Lane Kelley. July 1986. "The American Manager in Mexico: A Managerial Dilemma," *Massey Journal of Asian and Pacific Business*, (New Zealand). 2, 2.

Whatley, Arthur and Eva Kraus. June 1990. "Using Organization Development Technology in Mexico: Issues and Problems," *International Journal of Management.* 7, 2.

Woodworth, W. and R. Nelson. 1980. "Information in Latin American Organization: Some Cautions," *Management International Review.* 20, 2.

Index

Acknowledgment letters, 81-82
Advertising, 45
Agriculture
    irrigation and, 19,24,26,37
    land distribution and, 25,26,29
    Ordaz administration and, 27
    pre-columbian period, 19-20
    products exported, 35,37
Air travel, 54
Alvarez, Luis Escheverría, 27
Announcement letters, 82
Apology letters, 80-81
Architecture, 12
Arts
    popular culture, 11-13
    pre-Columbian period, 20
Aztecs
    empire of, 14-15
    pre-Columbian period, 20

Banks, banking
    1980s crisis in, 27-28
    Brady Agreement of 1989 and,
        29-30
    first national bank and, 21,39
    International Bank of Mexico and,
        25
    NAFTA (North American Free
        Trade Agreement)
        expectations and, 30
Body language, 70,77
Borrowing, 70
Brady Agreement of 1989, 29-30
Breweries, 39-40
Business
    American impatience and, 65-66
    apology letters and, 80-81

business letters and, 75-76,78-79
communication etiquette in, 62-68
credit, collection letters and, 80
deference and, 62-63
family connections and, 4-5
fatalism vs. sense of control and,
    61-62,70-71,97
goodwill letters and, 81-82
historical concepts and, 16-17
holidays and, 115-117
information organizations on,
    55-56
information specificity differences
    and, 60-61,67-68,95
letters of introduction and, 79
memoranda and, 82-83
perception of United States and,
    71-74
quality control in, 61-62,97
sales letters and, 79-80
social aspect of, 59-60,106-108
time perception differences and,
    57-59,60-61,70,95
United States people speaking
    Spanish in, 75-77
    See also Entertaining;
        Management

Calles, Plutarco Elías, 24,52
Camacho, Manuel Avila, 25
CANACINTRA. See National
    Chamber of Processing
    Industries (CANACINTRA)
Candlemas Day, 116
Cárdenas, Lázaro, 24-25,38,47
Case histories
    on communications, 69
    on entertaining, 103

Economy
  (1877-1911) Díaz Presidential
    period and, 22-23
  (1928-1934) Calles administration
    and, 24
  (1934-1940) Cárdenas
    administration and, 24-25
  (1940-1946) Camacho's
    administration and, 25
  (1946-1952) Valdés administration
    and, 26
  (1952-1958) Cortines
    administration and, 26
  (1958-1960) Mateos
    administration and, 26-27
  (1964-1970) Ordaz administration
    and, 27
  (1970-1976) Alvarez
    administration and, 27
  (1976-1982) Portillo
    administration and, 28
  (1982-1988) Madrid
    administration and, 28
  (1988-present) Gortari
    administration and, 28-32
  first national bank and, 21,39
  international trade and, 40-41
  labor issues and, 45-47
  Maquiladora (Border
    Industrialization Program
    [PIF]) and, 41-45,99-100
  present and future, 32
  statistics on, 33,49
  stock market and, 49-51
  transportation and, 51-54
  See also Industry
Energy, 55-56
Entertaining
  business discussions and, 106-108
  case history of, 103
  "do and don't" list, 110-113
  social acceptability, 113-115
  table manners and, 103-110,111
  See also Society, social life
European Community, (EC), 47-48

Family
  children and, 3
  father and, 2-3
  godparents and, 3
  home-based hospitality and, 71
  vs. individuality, 2-5,13,100-101
  vs. job, 99
  male-female relations in, 5-6
  marriage and, 5-6
  women and, 4
Farming. *See* Agriculture
Fatalism, 61-62,70-71,97
FDN. *See* National Democratic Front
  (FDN)
Fishing, 37
Forestry, 37

GATT. *See* General Agreement on
  Tariffs and Trade (GATT)
General Agreement on Tariffs and
  Trade (GATT), 47-48
Geography, 35
Gerrera, José Joaquín de, 21
Godparents, 3
Goodwill letters, 81-82
Gortari, Salinas de
  domestic policy of (cities), 7
  economic policy of, 28-32
  NAFTA and, 48-49
  party affiliation of, 33
Guadalajara
  city, region of, 8
  industry in, 39
  population, density of, 34
Guatemala, 20
Guerrero, Vicente, 21

Haciendas (estates), 20,23,29
Hairstyles, 89
Hidalgo, Miguel, 21
Hidden Differences (Hall), 58
Highways, 26,53-54
History
  1970s (the lost years) and, 27-28
  Aztec culture and, 14-15